CW00402675

NO ROSES AROUND THE DOOR
A Black Comedy
by Simon Bamford

AUTHOR'S INTRODUCTION - IMPORTANT

Be warned... "No Roses Around the Door" is not a suitable "Church Hall Drama"... "Roses" is a deep exploration of human kind, human attitudes, human failings. I would recommend that it be billed as "Not suitable for children", but in my experience, I find that to refer to the "narrow minded adult" as superior to a child would be an insult to the intelligence of children.

"Roses" is about people, all people, their prejudices, their weaknesses, their judgements, their lies, their truths. My writings have always explored man's inhumanity towards man and "Roses" is no exception. "Roses" is not a "gay" play, nor is it "heavy drama". Violence is a serious issue, an issue that many of us have to face at one time in our lives, many throughout our lives. However, it has to be realised that every situation, however brutal, would be sprinkled with humour. Life is like that, there's no escaping. At times humour can be more hurtful than a physical blow.

Simon Bamford.

Please return to
the
Maddermarket
Theatre

CHARACTERS in order of appearance

DAVID JACKSON - David is a man in his fifties, a white collar worker who lives under the threat of redundancy. He has a passion for jigsaw puzzles. He is tolerant in his manner but with a temper that blows hot and cold. He is a home loving man, sometimes irritatingly so.

SALLY JACKSON - Sally is David's long suffering wife. She is also in her fifties, slightly overweight. She can be very judgemental and cynical in her opinions. She is bored with her life, marriage and especially her husband.

JASON JACKSON - Jason is twenty two, the son of David and Sally. Jason is unemployed but has ways and means of supporting himself. His relationship with Sally is very close but slightly strained towards David. He gives the impression of being tough and street-wise, but underneath there lurks a Jason that he hides from his parents, or does he?

JENNY JACKSON *(Off-stage Voice)* - Jenny is the daughter, twenty six, she is a nurse in the Casualty Department of the local hospital.

DETECTIVE INSPECTOR WYATT - Wyatt is a tall man of a quiet studious nature, not the stereo type detective. He dresses in plain clothes of a sober fashion, looking more like an undertaker than a policeman.

CONSTABLE PERKINS - Perkins is approximately thirty. He wears uniform. His manner is polite and given the circumstances of the play slightly inexperienced to deal with the situation. Perkins originates from a small Norfolk village. His accent is not the stereo-type Norfolk drawl, but his speech is rather slow and thoughtful, giving the impression that he is lacking in education. A married man with seven children, all boys.

PETER BLACK - Peter is homosexual, although nothing in his appearance or mannerisms would indicate this, nor is his voice camp in any way. He is a strikingly good-looking man who dresses in suit and necktie of the office worker mode. His manner is normally quiet, kind, wise and generous, but given the situation, he is under considerable stress that has rendered him almost exhausted.

SETTING

A typical lounge of a middle class suburban house, situated in any small town in England. There are two entrances, one leading to the stairs and front door, and one leading to the kitchen. A window looks out onto the front garden.

The furnishings are typical, three piece suite, dining room suite, etc. On the table is a jigsaw puzzle of a country cottage. Around the door of the cottage there are roses. At the opening of the play the puzzle is incomplete. Scattered over the table are the remaining pieces, some of which have to be inserted during the first act of the play. This can be achieved by numbering the pieces for easy identification by the actors. At the opening of Act Two, a large section of the puzzle has been completed, this can be achieved by having two identical puzzles, one to replace the other.

ACT I

It is 9.45 pm on a Friday evening in October 1990. DAVID is sitting at the table doing a jigsaw puzzle. SALLY is reading the local newspaper.

DAVID: *(Softly)* A blue bit with a little bit of black. *(SALLY noisily turns pages of newspaper)* Blue with a little bit of black.

SALLY: Must you keep talking to yourself?

DAVID: Sorry.

SALLY: I'm trying to read the paper.

DAVID: Can't see that my quiet mumbles are a distraction!

SALLY: Well they are. *(Parrot fashion)* "A little bit of black with a little bit of blue". Drives me up the wall.

DAVID: Sorry. I'll try not to.

Silence

SALLY: Fancy that.

DAVID: Fancy what?

SALLY: The Pearson's, two doors up, got nicked for not having a tele licence.

DAVID: Really?

SALLY: Yes, really. It's here in the paper. My God, what a showing up. Two flash cars in the garden and no tele licence.

DAVID: Perhaps they just forgot.

SALLY: Fined seventy pounds. Ridiculous! Not much more than the cost of the licence anyhow.

DAVID: That'll be on top of buying a licence.

SALLY: Yes, I suppose you're right. Haven't you finished that yet?

DAVID: Lord, no. This is a hard one. Hardest I've ever had I think... No... that one of York Minster was a bit of a bastard. I'm sure there are bits missing. Blue with a touch of black. I've been through every piece and there's not one blue piece with a bit of black.

SALLY: How exciting. *(Yawns)* Jigsaws. Other men would be down at the pub on a Friday night, but not mine. Jigsaws. Like a big kid.

DAVID: It helps to relax me. And you wouldn't have this nice home and holidays abroad if I were to prop up the bar every night. You should think yourself lucky.

SALLY: *(Softly)* I'd think myself lucky if I could get through an evening without a bit of blue with a little bit of black.

DAVID: *(Excited)* Ah, here it is. *(Inserts piece)* Now, black with a little bit of blue. *(SALLY sighs loudly and returns to reading the newspaper. DAVID continues to concentrate on the puzzle. Apart from his soft mumblings and Sally rustling the paper they do not speak for at least thirty seconds)*

SALLY: *(Casually)* There's been another one of those beatings.

DAVID: *(Casually)* Beatings?

SALLY: Yes. Down Samson Lane. *(Reads)* "A forty year old man was attacked by a gang of youths in the early hours of Wednesday morning. The man, as yet unnamed, was approached in Samson Lane by a light-haired youth who asked for directions. The youth lured the man into Samson Lane woods where he was attacked from behind. The victim said, There were at least three of them, and was unable to give a positive description. The assailants robbed the man of his wallet containing thirty five pounds and various credit cards. The man was admitted to hospital with bruising and a head wound that required thirteen stitches. Police are continuing with their enquiries."

DAVID: Why did he go into the woods?

SALLY: Pardon?

DAVID: It said, he was lured into the woods by the youth. What for?

SALLY: It doesn't say, but it's obvious why.

DAVID: Is it?

SALLY: Yes. He was queer.

DAVID: Who was?

SALLY: The bloke with the busted head.

DAVID: How do you know?

SALLY: That's where they go. Samson Lane woods.

DAVID: Who do?

SALLY: Queers.

DAVID: *(Finding a piece)* Ah, here you are you little blighter... How do you know?

SALLY: Jason told me.

DAVID: How does he know of such things?

SALLY: Because he goes out now and then. You know, meets people. Indulges in conversation, opening and shutting his mouth. Socialising. Not everyone sits at home doing jigsaws.

DAVID: *(Finding the piece)* Ah. In you go... Don't know about now and then... it's every night... Pity he don't go out during the day and get himself a job. *(A silence)*

SALLY: It's called queer bashing.

DAVID: What is?

SALLY: *(Sighs)* Bashing queers.

DAVID: Oh... Black with a line and a little touch of blue... Don't like that word.

SALLY: What word?

DAVID: Queer... I prefer gay.

SALLY: I suppose that's what Peter prefers to be called is it?

DAVID: Peter prefers to be called Peter.

SALLY: But he's queer?

DAVID: Gay!

SALLY: How did you find out?

DAVID: Find out what?

SALLY: That Peter was queer?

DAVID: Gay!

SALLY: That Peter was gay?

DAVID: He told me.

SALLY: Why?

DAVID: Why is he gay or why did he tell me?

SALLY: Why did he tell you?

DAVID: Because I asked him.

SALLY: You? You asked him if he was gay? You of all people?

DAVID: Well I didn't actually ask and he didn't actually say it. It sort of became obvious. *(Finds another piece)* In you go... Not married, well into his forties, not that that means anything... It just seemed somehow I knew and he knew I knew... Doesn't make any difference to me... Still the same Peter... straight or gay.

SALLY: Has he ever...?

DAVID: Ever what?

SALLY: You know... tried anything?

DAVID: Tried anything?

SALLY: On you?

DAVID: Don't be so ignorant woman. Just because he's that way doesn't mean he's after every man he meets.

SALLY: I thought that sort... Gays... do?

DAVID: Look, Peter is a friend. What his sexual preferences are does not affect that friendship. As far as I'm concerned, Peter is a happily married man just like me. Only difference, his wife happens to be a man. Now look, can we change the subject?

SALLY: What shall we discuss then? Jigsaws? *(A silence)* Have you ever met her, him?

DAVID: Who?

SALLY: Peter's wife, boyfriend, whatever?

DAVID: No.

SALLY: Does he speak about him?... You know... like when you speak about your wife?... Or do you never talk about me in the office?

DAVID: In an unspoken way, yes he does.

SALLY: I would find that very difficult.

DAVID: What?

SALLY: Having a conversation with a limp-wristed queer.

DAVID: Peter is not limp-wristed.

SALLY: I expect he's camp though?

DAVID: Where on earth do you get this terminology from? And no, Peter is not the least bit camp, and why do you insist on putting labels on everyone and everything? It's futile. Especially as you don't even know the man.

SALLY: As far as I'm concerned they get the labels they deserve. *(Holds up the paper)* And as for this pervert, what can he expect, taking young boys into the woods. Disgusting. All the same these queers.

DAVID: There you go again. Another label, another assumption. A man was beaten and robbed and you assume he deserves it simply because you've decided you know all about his sexual habits.

SALLY: Samson woods is known for it.

DAVID: Is there anything else in that paper we can discuss?

SALLY: The unemployment figures are up again. Want to discuss them?

DAVID: Would do a lot more good if you were to pop upstairs and ask our dear son what he's going to do to reduce them. If only by one.

SALLY: And perhaps if you were to pop upstairs to talk to him he'd faint away.

DAVID: And what is that meant by that?

SALLY: When have you ever shown any interest in what he wants to do? All you do is constantly get at the boy to get a job. Never mind what kind of job, as long as it's a job.

DAVID: The only job he's interested in is no job.

SALLY: That's so typical of you. Always putting him down. You've no idea how sensitive he is to your constant griping.

DAVID: About as sensitive as hobnailed boots. And what's his latest pie-in-the-sky, get-rich-quick idea? What bright new horizon is being painted for him by this so-called Zak friend of his?

SALLY: He's learning a great deal working for Zak. Zak says he's going to set up an outlet in town and he's almost promised Jason that there'll be a manager's job for him... Zak says Jason has a flair for Men's fashion.

DAVID: Working on the Sunday market selling substandard, made in Bangladesh shirts, for some Pakistani for cash-in-hand, does not make him Hardy Amis.

SALLY: See what I mean? Always putting him down. Zak wouldn't pay him so well if his prospects were not looking up.

DAVID: When you're in the gutter, up is the only direction to look.

SALLY: You sicken me... Get on with your puzzle... *(Continues to read)*... Perhaps that's what you'd like him to be... a professional puzzle doer.

DAVID: Be better than selling stolen goods.

SALLY: *(Rustles paper in irritation)* There's enough of them hanging in your wardrobe.

A short silence.

DAVID: Black with a touch of green.

SALLY: Oh do shut up.

A short silence.

DAVID: Pity he didn't take a leaf out of Jenny's book.

SALLY: *(Slams paper down)* I've been waiting for that... Do you realise how many times in the course of a week you say that? I'm sure if we had a budgie the first thing you'd teach it to say is "Leaf out of Jenny's book. Leaf out of Jenny's book."

DAVID: Very droll I'm sure. All the same it's true.

SALLY: Jenny and Jason are as different as chalk and cheese and you know it.

DAVID: Yes one's a worker and one's a lay-about.

SALLY: He tries. But you wouldn't know about that, would you?

A silence.

DAVID: One thing I do know, Jenny had ambition, always did. Ten years old she was. Sat on my knee and said, "Daddy, I'm going to be a nurse". There was such a look of determination in those young eyes that I knew, even at that tender age, Jenny had planned her future. "I'm going to be a nurse". And by George, she meant it and she did it.

SALLY: She also said she was going to be a ballet dancer, a pop star, a film star, a model... Oh yes, and the fastest typist in the world so she could write books quicker than Barbara Cartland.

DAVID: The girl had ambition.

SALLY: Dreams!

DAVID: Well at least one of those dreams came true.

SALLY: If you think working a twelve hour night shift in the Casualty Department is a dream come true, you must have some very peculiar dreams.

DAVID: And what dreams does he have? Apart from lying on his back all day and wandering the streets at night with his so-called mates... And as for this Zak, who ever he is, why doesn't he give him a proper job if he thinks so highly of him?

SALLY: I just told you, he's opening up a shop...

DAVID: Come on woman, use a bit of sense. What kind of legitimate business man would allow his employees to break the law?

SALLY: Break the law?

DAVID: Yes. The boy is claiming dole money. He's not allowed to have a Sunday job and not declare it... He'll get caught, you mark my words... Then it'll be us that gets the showing up.

SALLY: Showing up?

DAVID: When it hits the paper... Never mind about no tele licence... We're talking embezzlement here... Fraud... Could make front page.

SALLY: Thousands do it.

DAVID: And thousands get caught... Where will Zak and his promises be then?

JASON enters, wearing jeans, red tee-shirt, trainer shoes and an expensive black leather jacket. He walks to the table. Moves jigsaw pieces around with his finger.

JASON: *(Casually)* Did I hear Zak's name mentioned? *(Inserts a piece of puzzle)*

DAVID: Do you mind? I've been looking for that bit.

JASON: Well I've just found it for you. *(Picks up another piece, inserts it)* And there's another. Well did I?

DAVID: Did you what?

JASON: Hear Zak's name mentioned?

SALLY: Yes you did. Your father thinks he's a crook

DAVID: I never said no such thing.

SALLY: You implied it.

JASON: A crook?

DAVID: I didn't say he was. I said you were.

JASON: *(Picks up another piece, inserts it)* How's that?

DAVID: Fiddling the dole. They'll catch up with you, you know. They send inspectors to them sort of places looking for people like you.

JASON: Not on a Sunday.

DAVID: Of course they do.

JASON: Double time Sunday... Cost too much... Everyone's looking to cut costs these days, you should know that... How's the redundancy situation going at the Tax Office?... Think you'll get it?

DAVID: No.

JASON: Let me know if you do. *(Picks up a piece, inserts it)* I'll get you set up on the market.

DAVID: Will you stop doing that please.

JASON: Doing what?

DAVID: Doing my jigsaw.

SALLY: Told you he'd make a good jigsaw doer.

A silence. JASON walks away, turns slowly.

JASON: Dad...

DAVID: What?

JASON: I don't suppose you could lend me a fiver?

DAVID: You suppose right.

JASON: Oh come on. I'll pay you back.

DAVID: Terrific. I lend you a fiver and you'll pay me back. Is that just the fiver or all the other included?

JASON: What other?

DAVID: The twenty or thirty thousand you've borrowed over the years and never paid back. Even though you promised, sometimes on your Mother's life you would?

JASON: *(To Sally)* Why does he always exaggerate?

SALLY: Because he's dull. Dull people do that. It puts a bit of colour into their lives.

JASON: I don't suppose you could see your way to...?

SALLY: Get my bag.

JASON: Thanks Mum.

DAVID: *(Stands. Angry)* You'll do no such thing. *(To Sally)* You do realise you're undermining my authority?

JASON: *(Laughs)* Authority?

DAVID: Yes, authority.

JASON: I'm twenty two years old. You have no authority over me. If Mum wants to lend me a fiver, then it's up to her. She can do what she likes with her money.

DAVID: It's not her money. It's my money. I had to work for that and I suggest if you want some you do the same thing.

SALLY: *(Firmly)* Get my bag Jason.

DAVID: And I said no.

SALLY: And I said yes...

DAVID: If you can afford to throw away five pound notes on a lay-about like him, perhaps I should start thinking of cutting you short.

SALLY: *(Rises and gets her bag)* Do that. You do that. *(Takes a five pound note from her purse)* And while you're about it, you'd better pop into the supermarket and buy the groceries so you can cook them when you get home. Here Jason. *(She hands him five pounds)* And don't forget to buy detergent. You'll need it to wash your clothes with and you may as well break up your kiddies puzzle because you won't have time after you've done the ironing and the hoovering for doing jigsaw puzzles.

DAVID: *(Shouts)* Why do you always side with him?

SALLY: *(Calmly)* For the same reason you always side with Jenny.

DAVID: I do not side with Jenny.

SALLY: Oh come on!

DAVID: I do not side with Jenny, do you hear. I just point out a few facts.

JASON: Facts?

DAVID: Jenny's got a job for a start.

JASON: So will I... Soon.

DAVID: Soon? Soon? You've been saying soon since you were sixteen.

JASON: *(In temper)* You know something? I get sick to death of hearing you harp on and on as though I just sit around and do nothing.

DAVID: But that's exactly what you do do.

JASON: Every Sunday I'm out there on that market. Five in the morning till nine at night. All weathers. And I work. Work my nuts off. I go to the job centre three times a week. I get enough crap off them without coming home to hear it from you as well. But then you're just like them. Sitting in your office all day then coming home to your jigsaws. You lot don't realise what it's like out there. Out there in the real world. You sit smugly on your fat arses judging. "There's plenty of jobs", you say. "Don't want to work". What you ought to do is go down that centre, have a look, see what's on offer. Oh yes, they have hundreds of cards pinned up, but the reality of it is they only need one.

"Slaves required to work for a pittance". Any good job, and I will admit there are occasions when one does appear, you can expect to stand in line with two or three hundred other guys hoping, not to get the job, just to be lucky enough to get an interview. I hope you do get made redundant and you have to go through it... I hope you have to sit in front of some smug little bastard who'll hand you your Giro, tell you to write letters, make phone calls and then you'll realise that the Post Office and British Telecom are not charitable organisations.

DAVID: I am not going to be made redundant.

JASON: When it comes to being a father you've been redundant for years.

DAVID: *(Almost screaming and banging his fists down onto the table causing pieces to jump onto the floor)* What? What? What? You ungrateful swine... Now look what you've made me do.

SALLY: You'd better go where ever you're going Jason... What must the neighbours think.

JASON moves to the door. DAVID rushes and blocks his exit. He is furious.

DAVID: Sod the neighbours. And you're not going anywhere, until you apologise.

JASON: Get out of my way Dad.

DAVID: Apologise.

SALLY: Stop it. I won't have the neighbours hearing all our business.

DAVID: He's not going anywhere until he withdraws that remark and, if you're so concerned about the neighbours, why don't you nip round and offer to buy them a tele licence with my money? That should keep them happy.

SALLY: You vicious pig.

DAVID: Yes, a vicious pig that sired a lazy, ungrateful piglet.

JASON: *(Turns his head to Sally, laughs)* The man's nuts.

DAVID grabs him violently by the collar of his jacket, pulls him across the room and throws him into the chair.

DAVID: Nuts? Nuts? I'll give you nuts.

SALLY: Leave him alone.

DAVID: Shut up.

JASON: *(Hissing)* Leave it out, Dad. You'll be sorry.

DAVID: Don't you threaten me, do you hear? Don't you ever threaten me.

JASON: Leave it...

   DAVID slaps him hard across the head.

DAVID: Apologise.

   JASON glares at him. He hits him again.

SALLY: Stop it David. For God's sake, stop it.

DAVID: Apologise.

   JASON glares, DAVID glares back. DAVID raises his hand to strike.

JASON: *(Softly)* Sorry. *(He lowers his eyes)*

DAVID: Sorry for what?

SALLY: He's said he's sorry, what more do you want?

DAVID: *(Thrusting out his hand)* The money.

JASON: *(Weakly)* But Mum gave it to...

DAVID: The money.

SALLY: I gave him that. You've no right.

DAVID: *(Shouting)* The money. Now.

SALLY: Keep it, Jason.

DAVID: *(Softly, threateningly)* Give me that money or I'll tear that fancy jacket from your back and take my belt to you.

   JASON slowly puts his hand into his pocket and hands David the five pound note.

JASON: You bastard.

DAVID: *(Grabs him by the jacket)* What!?

JASON: Mind the gear. Mind the gear.

DAVID: *(Releases him, throwing him back into the chair)* Mind the gear? Mind the gear? What I'd like to know is, where did the gear come from, eh?

JASON: Are you calling me a thief?

DAVID: That jacket. Cost at least a hundred and fifty to two hundred pounds, that I know of, so how come you tart around in something that most, honest working folk can't afford?

JASON: *(Loud)* I worked for this.

DAVID: Worked? Worked?

SALLY: Leave the boy alone.

DAVID: You wouldn't care if he walked in here wearing the crown jewels, as long as he said he worked for them.

JASON: Zak gave it to me.

DAVID: Zak? Zak? Balls to Zak. Do you honestly expect me to believe that he gave you a two hundred pound jacket for one days work? He may have come up the river on a banana boat, but I didn't.

JASON: It wasn't a days work, it was a weeks work, for your information. And a jacket like this may cost a couple in the shops, but that's not what he paid for it. It cost him no more than thirty quid, if that.

DAVID: Yes. I expect stolen goods are pretty cheap. *(DAVID turns away from him)*

Silence.

JASON: *(Softly)* Can I go?

DAVID: Go? Go where?

JASON: Out.

DAVID: Out?

JASON: Yes out... I'm meeting someone.

DAVID: At ten o'clock at night?

JASON: Yes.

DAVID: Who?

JASON: My business.

SALLY: He's twenty two years old, he can go where he likes and with who he likes.

DAVID: He's living in this house. He'll abide by the rules of this house.

SALLY: Rules?

DAVID: Yes, rules. I don't want him sneaking in and out, especially in the early hours... What's he up to I ask myself?... No good, I'll bet.

SALLY: You know something? You make me sick. You should just hear yourself sometimes. Talk about a loving father. The reason you see him as black is because you spend all your time painting him black... Now what I suggest you do is give him that money. My money. And then forget it all happened... We're a family. Families should stick together. You've got to realise it's not easy for the boy... You know yourself how difficult it is for the unemployed... Your father, for instance... When I met you, you were nothing but concerned for your dad because he couldn't find a job. Now your son's in the same boat and it's harder now... And who knows... You might be in that boat if those consultants decide to close your department down... You said last night you were worried sick about it... So come on... Calm down...

DAVID: *(Shrugs, hands Jason the note)* All I ask is a little respect.

JASON: Thanks Dad. *(Stands)* Sorry, I didn't mean...

DAVID: Yes, me too.

JASON: Sorry.

DAVID: Lot on my mind... Redundancies and...

JASON: Yes... I must go... *(Moves to door)* See you in the dole queue. *(Laughs)*

DAVID: Where can you possibly be going at this time of night?

JASON: Out... *(Looks at watch)* Have to go. I'm late.

DAVID: Late for what?

JASON: I'm meeting someone.

SALLY: A date?

JASON: *(Slowly)* Yes.

SALLY: That's nice.

DAVID: A date at ten o'clock?

JASON: Yes. What's wrong with that?

DAVID: When I was courting your Mother, I had to have her home by this time! Any later and I would have had her father chasing me down the street.

JASON: Yes. Well. Fathers are more open minded now. Well, some of them are. *(Exits)*

DAVID: *(Pauses. Turns, moves to table)* I suppose he meant that of me?

SALLY: What time is it?

DAVID: Just turned ten. *(Softly)* Never understand the young. Never seem to go out until it's time to come home. I blame the parents.

SALLY: Who's parents?

DAVID: Everyone's parents. When we were young, you had to be home by now... And why? Because that's what your father wanted and we respected that... Kids today don't know the meaning of respect.

SALLY: Rubbish... Respect is not measured by the hands of the clock... You have to earn respect.

DAVID: If I'd spoken to my father the way Jason just spoke to me, well I'd have finished up in the hospital.

SALLY: That's not respect. That's fear.

DAVID: *(A thoughtful pause)* Yes... I agree... You're right... *(Sits. Continues to do puzzle)* I can remember the day you told me you were pregnant. I sat down and I said to myself, "David," I said, "you're going to be a father. Make sure you don't make the same mistakes as he did."

SALLY: And did you?

DAVID: Did I what?

SALLY: Make the same mistakes?

DAVID: No, of course not... "My son," I said, "will not be ruled with an iron fist... but with love and kindness... My son will look on me as a friend..." But that was a mistake right from the start... Assuming I would father a son... Funny how men never think their first born will turn out to be female.

SALLY: Was it so disappointing?

DAVID: Don't be daft... I was so proud of Jenny... still am.

SALLY: What about Jason?

DAVID: The second is different... The initial shock of being a father has gone... I know what you're saying, thinking, but look at him. I want to be proud of him, but he makes it very difficult, especially when you compare him to Jenny.

SALLY: *(Softly)* That's an awful thing to say.

DAVID: *(Softly)* Yes, I know... but true.

A silence, he inserts pieces into puzzle. She stands. Moves over to David. Looks at puzzle.

SALLY: Nice.

DAVID: Yes.

SALLY: *(Picks up puzzle box)* That's what I would like.

DAVID: What?

SALLY: *(Wraps arms around her body, moves away)* A cottage in the country. Thatched roof... Roses round the door.

DAVID: When I suggested roses round our door you said "No". Said the thorns would catch your clothes.

SALLY: Here's different... A cottage without roses just isn't a cottage... *(Sighs)* Oh what a life... I'm bored... Bored...

DAVID: Watch tele or something.

SALLY: I'm not that kind of bored.

DAVID: Come and do some of this.

SALLY: That would turn my boredom into depression. No thank you.

DAVID: Times were you loved a good jigsaw. *(Looks up, smiles reminiscently)* When we were young... before the kids... Remember that game you invented... Strip jigsaw... Every tenth bit you found meant the loser had to remove something... *(Coyly)* Care for a game now?

SALLY: Don't be so silly.

DAVID: Time's were when you couldn't wait for a game... Especially when you adapted the rules so the winner got to remove the loser's shirt, trousers, whatever... I used to cheat you know... Lose on purpose.

SALLY: I was aware of that.

DAVID: Come on... it'll be fun.

SALLY: No... Don't be disgusting.

DAVID: You couldn't wait to get them off me... Right little hot arse... The hungry look in your eyes... Waiting for the last bit to come off.

SALLY: *(Embarrassed)* We were young... And you were worth looking at.

DAVID: Thank you.

SALLY: Sorry... I didn't mean... Yes I did... It was new to me... I'd never seen... You know?

DAVID: And now it's old and withered. Not worth a second glance?

SALLY: Not just you... me too... Look at us... We had beautiful bodies and I suppose we thought we always would have... But then one day you look in the mirror and there it is... Old age creeping up... Cute imperfections changing into horrendous eyesores... Everything turning limp and sagging... We should have taken more care.

DAVID: I still find you very attractive Sally.

SALLY: Do you?

DAVID: Of course... And if you were to come and play, I'd make damned sure I was the winner.

SALLY: Would you?

DAVID: Of course...

SALLY: I'm touched, but later.

DAVID: Later?

SALLY: *(Kisses him lightly)* Yes, later. Would you like a hot drink or something?

DAVID: I'd like a game of strip jigsaw.

SALLY: And a bucket to throw up in... Cocoa or coffee?

DAVID: Coffee.

SALLY smiles and exits. DAVID continues to do the jigsaw. He looks up, smiles, laughs. SALLY enters.

SALLY: Kettle's on... Are you hungry?

DAVID: *(Looks up, laughs)* Not half.

SALLY: For something to eat... I don't know, the older you get, the worse you get... I fancy a Chinese.

DAVID: Is that man or meal?

SALLY: A chicken curry... I could murder a chicken curry.

DAVID: What time do they close?

SALLY: Oh not until very late on a Friday.

DAVID: *(Stands and moves to window)* Two chicken curries with rice then a re-run of the Karma Sutra... It's raining... Better take the car. *(Exits to the hall)*

SALLY: *(Calls)* I'd better turn the kettle off till you get back.

DAVID: *(Off)* Have you seen my car keys?

SALLY: You had them last.

DAVID: *(Entering)* I hung them on the hook.

SALLY: Did you check your jacket?

DAVID: *(Looking around room)* Yes. Not there. Felt sure I hung them on the hook.

SALLY: Perhaps you've left them in the car.

DAVID: No.

SALLY: Well they're not here. Go and check.

He mumbles and exits. SALLY exits to the kitchen. She returns. DAVID storms in.

DAVID: It's gone. The car's gone. That little sod has taken my car.

END OF ACT I

ACT II

Two hours later. On the coffee table there are two plates containing the remains of a chicken curry, two earthenware mugs and two glasses containing a small amount of water. The jigsaw pieces on the floor have been replaced onto the table and quite a large amount of the puzzle has been completed. This can be achieved by having two identical puzzles.

DAVID enters. He is wearing pyjamas, dressing gown and slippers, his hair is a mess. He looks anxious. Moves to the window, looks out, mumbles.

DAVID: Cheeky sod... Damned nerve of the boy... Don't suppose he'll even think of putting petrol in... *(Moves away from window, goes to table, sits, smiles)* She thinks I cheated... Well not this time. *(Inserts piece into puzzle)* Just need new glasses.

SALLY enters. She too is wearing a dressing gown and slippers. Under the gown is a pink nightdress.

SALLY: Are you coming back to bed?

DAVID: Not yet.

SALLY: I'd better clear these things away. *(Picks up plates)*

DAVID: Leave it till morning.

SALLY: Can't do that... It smells.

DAVID: Well leave it for now... Come and give me a kiss.

SALLY: *(Moving to him, smiling shyly)* Goodness, there's no holding you, is there?

DAVID: *(Grabs her, pulls her close)* Come here you gorgeous creature. *(Pulls her onto lap)*

SALLY: Stop it you fool. Jason may walk in.

DAVID: You didn't think of that when you were on a winning streak. *(Kisses her)*

SALLY: *(Stands)* I didn't mean what I said you know... about your body... It's still very pretty.

DAVID: Pretty?

SALLY: Yes pretty... I hate hairy men, don't you?

DAVID: *(Wryly)* Well actually I find them irresistible.

SALLY: You know what I mean... I'd better clear these plates away. *(Picks up plates, stops, giggles)* Can you imagine the look on his face?

DAVID: Whose face?

SALLY: Jason, if he had walked in on us?

DAVID: We are married... It is allowed you know.

SALLY: All the same, what would you have done? Sitting there without a stitch on, doing a jigsaw as though your life depended upon it.

DAVID: I don't know... What would you have done?

SALLY: Quite calmly asked him to ring for a doctor as you were having one of your funny turns.

DAVID: And what would you have done if he walked in and caught us down there? *(Points to the carpet)*

SALLY: Simply raised my head and screamed, "Rape!" *(Exits with plates)*

DAVID continues to do the puzzle. SALLY returns.

DAVID: That was quick.

SALLY: I'll wash them in the morning... You coming up?

DAVID: No, not yet.

SALLY: Come on, leave that, you can finish it tomorrow night. *(Smiles, moves to table)* I'll play you your five pieces to my ten... *(Runs finger over puzzle lightly)* Did you cheat?

DAVID: No.

SALLY: Bet you did.

DAVID: I did not.

SALLY: It really turns you on, doesn't it?

DAVID: What?

SALLY: Losing? Being exposed?

DAVID: Are you objecting?

SALLY: I'm just wondering what you get up to in the park?

DAVID: Eh?

SALLY: And you did buy a new raincoat last month.

DAVID: What are you on about?

SALLY: *(Moves away)* Forget it. Joke. Exposure.. Raincoat. *(Picks up glasses and mugs. Looks at him. He is frowning)* Flasher! In your raincoat!.. *(Exit)*

DAVID: *(Still frowning watches her exit. Shrugs)* Well what's wrong with wanting to look smart? *(Continues to do puzzle. Stops. Looks up. Frowns)* Flasher?... Oh... Joke... Stupid bitch... *(Shouts through)* At least I've got something worth looking at.

SALLY: *(Entering)* That's what you think.

DAVID: Since when have you been an expert on the male anatomy?

SALLY: I spend a lot of time in the park... Are you coming to bed?

DAVID: No. I'm waiting for our dear son so I can give him a piece of my mind.

SALLY: He may not be in till two or three, you know what he's like.

DAVID: I don't care if he's out all night, it's not him I'm worrying about, it's my car. I'll not sleep until I know it's safely back in our driveway... I'm waiting. *(SALLY sits on the sofa)* I thought you were going to bed?

SALLY: No, I'll wait with you.

DAVID: No need.

SALLY: Oh yes there is. I'm not going to be awakened at two or three in the morning to the sound of you two fighting.

DAVID: There'll be no fighting, I can assure you. *(Firmly)* There'll be no fighting... *(Softly)* Just murder... Go to your bed.

SALLY: No, besides I'm not tired... Want me to help you finish that?

DAVID: No thank you. I haven't got the energy. *(They both laugh)*

SALLY: Poor old man.

DAVID: *(Stands, moves around room)* This is nice, isn't it... like old times... before the kids. Hasn't it gone quick... Don't seem five minutes ago I was waiting outside your house on my pushbike. Your mother shouting, "Make sure you behave yourself young lady."... Remember how we'd wait until we got to the end of the street and around the corner? Onto my crossbar you'd jump and away we'd go... Off to the hills... and, oh my God, your father. The looks he gave me when I brought you home... He made me feel so guilty. Sometimes, you know, I was filled with an overwhelming desire to jump up and shout, "It wasn't me, Mr Marshall... it was her."

SALLY: Damned good job you didn't.

DAVID: *(As though talking to Sally's father)* Believe me sir, it was her. I try to stop her, sir. It was her. Always her. *(Swings around to face her. Slowly)* Still is.

SALLY: You know what this is called don't you?

DAVID: What?

SALLY: Second childhood.

DAVID: Just memories. Don't you ever travel down memory lane?

SALLY: Of course... but... We were different then... Young... Youth... Gone.. Now it's middle age waiting for old age... I expect when we're old we'll look back and think how different we are from now.

DAVID: I'm no different.

SALLY: Course you are...

DAVID: Only difference with me is, when I was young I could do everything twice.

SALLY: Only once now?

DAVID: Don't be rude... I know what you're after... You're after my insurance policy.

SALLY: *(Thoughtfully)* A rich widow... I could get myself a toy boy...

The telephone rings.

(TECHNICAL POINT: The voices on the other end of the line should be heard through the FX system. SALLY has to give the impression that she cannot hear the voices)

DAVID: Who on earth can that be at this time of night? *(Picks up the receiver)* Hello.

JENNY: Hello dad, it's me, Jenny.

DAVID: *(To Sally)* It's Jenny. *(Into the receiver)* Hello pet. Nothing wrong is there? Calling at this time.

JENNY: No... Well yes... Did I get you from your bed?

DAVID: No... No... We were just going. What's wrong pet?

JENNY: I'm all right, it's just... just. There's a man here who's in one hell of a state and you know him.

DAVID: Who?

JENNY: Peter. Peter from your office... The one who's gay.

DAVID: What's wrong with him?

JENNY: Nothing...

DAVID: But you said he was in one hell of a state.

SALLY: *(Jumping up)* Jason?

DAVID: *(To Sally)* No. No. It's Peter at work.

SALLY: Peter?

DAVID: Peter. *(Sally sits)* What's this to do with me pet? What's his problem. Has he been hurt?

JENNY: It's not him, it's his friend. A gang of thugs beat him up, pretty badly too. I've told Peter there's nothing he can do sitting around here. Phillip, that's his friend, is going to undergo surgery. They're getting him ready now. I've told Peter it will be six or seven hours before there's any news and that he ought to go somewhere and rest.

DAVID: Well that's understandable... him wanting to be there.

JENNY: It's not that simple. Phillip's parents have arrived. His father is not being too kind to Peter... Peter's very upset.

DAVID: But what can I do love?

JENNY: I thought you'd want to know... If I had waited till tomorrow the first thing you would have said is that I should have phoned you. He needs someone to talk to dad. He's in a mess. Couldn't you come down and sit with him?

DAVID: I haven't got the car. Jason took it.

JENNY: Oh... but... oh, Dad... He looks so sad. I can see him through the window... Phillip's mum and dad are in there too. Other side of the room, as far away from him as they can get.

DAVID: *(Thinking for a while)* Can you get him to the phone?

JENNY: I can try.

DAVID: Hang up love... talk to him... tell him who you are. Tell him you've spoken to me. Tell him to call me.

JENNY: What if he won't?

DAVID: Force him... If not you ring me back and we'll see what's to be done... How bad is his friend?

JENNY: Very bad... He's lost a lot of blood.

DAVID: Where did it happen?

JENNY: Samson Lane.

DAVID: Oh... Get him to ring me... Bye love.

JENNY: I'll try. Bye.

DAVID replaces the receiver. SALLY is looking decidedly concerned.

SALLY: Get who to ring you?

DAVID: Peter.

SALLY: Peter? Peter who?

DAVID: Peter from work. He's down at the hospital.

SALLY: Well, what's it all about? You've already told me he's down at the hospital.

DAVID: He needs someone to talk to.

SALLY: I don't understand. What are you on about?

DAVID: I'm going to ask him to come here.

SALLY: Here? When?

DAVID: Tonight of course.

SALLY: Tonight! It's gone twelve o'clock. What's his problem?

DAVID: His friend is just about to have an operation.

SALLY: Well? *(Raising her voice)* There are hundreds of people having operations, but we don't send out invitations to their friends and family.

DAVID: Jenny says he's in a state. I just knew you'd be full of compassion and understanding.

SALLY: *(Louder)* It's not the point of being compassionate or understanding. I want to know why he is coming here?

DAVID: Because I'm his friend and he needs someone to talk to.

SALLY: *(Shouts)* But what does he want to talk about? What's the problem?

DAVID: The problem is... is his friend... his lover, if you like, his wife, his husband, whatever, was beaten up tonight by a gang of thugs.

SALLY: Beaten up? Oh... I see... did he say where he was beaten up?

DAVID: Yes.

SALLY: Where?

DAVID: Samson Lane.

SALLY: I might have known it... I might have... Serves him bloody right.

DAVID: *(Angry)* Don't say that. No-one deserves that woman. Nobody.

SALLY: Don't shout. Anyway, it's pointless to argue over something that won't happen. He'll stay at the hospital.

DAVID: You don't understand. There's a problem down at the hospital for him. Phillip...

SALLY: *(Interrupting sharply)* Phillip? Who the hell is Phillip?

DAVID: His partner... Apparently his parents are there... and... I suppose they're making it rather uncomfortable for Peter.

SALLY: Well you can hardly blame them, can you?

DAVID: I'm not blaming anybody. I do not consider myself qualified to be judge and jury over other people, not like some that I know.

SALLY: I don't want him here in this house.

DAVID· Tough, because you're going to get him here. When he rings I'm going to invite him round. I'm a friend. He needs someone to talk to.

SALLY: And he's going to talk to you? This will be quite a historical event...

You playing the Samaritan... You ever thought about talking to us when we've got problems? Has that ever occurred to you? Maybe sit down and talk to your son? Help him?... We've already had a display of your Samaritanism tonight, haven't we?

DAVID: All I asked from him was a little bit of respect.

SALLY: And all I'm asking is for you to respect my wishes, that I don't want his sort here.

DAVID: What sort?

SALLY: Gay boys.

DAVID: Look. He's coming here to talk to me, not to take me to bed.

SALLY: Talking of bed, I think that's where I'll go. I'm not sitting around here... *(Moves to exit. Turns)* Oh, and if you offer him a coffee, make sure you wash the mug in boiling water when he's gone.

DAVID: Boiling water? What are you talking about?

SALLY: Aids dear. Aids.

DAVID: My God, you are so ignorant.

SALLY: I am not ignorant. I happen to read the papers.

DAVID:*(Laughing cynically)* You read the papers! *(Picks up newspaper)* You read this rag. A comic, not a newspaper, my dear!

SALLY: I'll have you know that that rag, as you care to call it, was the first paper to warn Britain that Aids would become an epidemic plague.

DAVID: And ten years ago we were all going to get Herpes, but we didn't.

SALLY: *(Moves into room)* I don't want him here. It makes me nervous. Why can't he sort out his own problems?

DAVID: My goodness woman. Can't you try to understand what it must be like for him down there.

SALLY: Why can't he go to his own home?

DAVID: He lives forty miles away... Anyway, you're probably right... he'll refuse to come, so you're worrying over nothing, but I can't ignore this situation.

SALLY: Well I can.

DAVID: Yes, you can. You can ignore it. You can go to your bed. You can leave it to me.

SALLY: Yes. I'll leave it to the good Samaritan... I expect you'll get in next year's honours list... The Samaritan of the year.

DAVID: If only you could hear yourself. If you could just listen to what you say.

SALLY: *(Softly)* I know what I say, all right. I know what I say... How do you know his friend doesn't deserve what he got? Hey?... How do you know he wasn't trying to seduce some innocent youth? But he got a nasty shock because the youth was a bit stronger than him? More than likely gave him the hiding he deserves?

DAVID: My God, that's a terrible thing to say. *(Firmly with anger)* I do not know what happened. And I am not in the ball game of making assumptions... Jenny said it was a gang of thugs.

SALLY: How does she know it was a gang of thugs?

DAVID: How the hell do I know how she knows?... Perhaps he told her.

SALLY: Well of course he would, wouldn't he?

DAVID: He must have been a pretty strong youth if he could put a man on the operating table... I do not want to judge anybody.

SALLY: Pity you can't learn to judge yourself. I'm going to my bed.

The telephone rings. They both look at each other.

DAVID: Go to bed.

SALLY: No.

DAVID picks up receiver.

DAVID: Hello.

PETER: *(Softly)* Hello David, it's Peter... I'm afraid I don't... Sorry, but I... This is so difficult.

DAVID: Peter, don't worry... I understand... Jenny told me what happened... I'm sorry Peter... Such a dreadful...

PETER: Yes... Yes...

DAVID: Jenny told you I wanted you to ring me?

PETER: Yes.

DAVID: Look Peter, we only live a mile or so away. Why don't you get in a taxi and come and...

PETER: No... No... Thank you. It's very good of you but I couldn't put you to so much bother...

DAVID: If it was any bother I wouldn't have told Jenny to get you to ring me... Look Peter, you can't do any good sitting down there by yourself... If anything happens, Jenny will ring and I can get you back there in ten minutes or so.

PETER: *(Breaking down)* Oh shit, shit... I'm sorry... But... I'm sorry... I don't know what to do... I'm sorry... His father said... my fault... It wasn't... I can't stay here...

DAVID: Peter... Peter... Please, I want you to come here.

PETER: *(Regaining control)* If you're sure it's okay... If you really don't mind I would appreciate it... But I'd rather walk... I need to be alone for a while.

DAVID: I understand... You know where we live?

PETER: Yes... Number six.

DAVID: Yes.

PETER: Thank you David... I can't thank you enough... I couldn't go home and sit waiting alone... God, they've almost killed him.

DAVID: Get a taxi Peter... I'll be waiting for you.

PETER: No, I'd rather walk.

DAVID: Well take care... It's bad enough... Sorry.

PETER: I'd better hang up now.

DAVID: Yes... I'll catch you later.

PETER: Yes... Thank you again David... Bye for now.

DAVID: Bye... Peter. *(Replaces receiver)*

SALLY: I don't understand you. I just don't understand you at all.

DAVID: I thought you were going to your bed?

SALLY: You were patronising him.

DAVID: Patronising?

SALLY: Yes... Why can't he find one of his own kind to comfort him?

DAVID: Peter does not happen to be what you'd likely call a mincing queen who ponces around gay night clubs... He's a man... Just a man who happens to be homosexual. It doesn't mean he has gay friends.

SALLY: I thought that sort hunted in packs.

DAVID: You are so narrow minded.

SALLY: And you're so vulnerable... *(Pause)* I've never understood why that man wants to be friends with you and, even more confusing, is your wanting to encourage his friendship in your direction... Unless, of course...

DAVID: Unless, of course, what?

SALLY: You're that way inclined as well.

DAVID: *(Loud)* What? What?

SALLY: Possible.

DAVID: But I'm married you stupid woman.

SALLY: Now who's narrow minded... Well... Are you?

DAVID: You know damned well I'm not.

SALLY: How am I supposed to know?

DAVID: After all these years of sharing the same bed, I should have thought that answers itself... I am not gay. But one thing I am and that's tolerant of other people's preferences... Live and let live, that's what I say... And I would like to think that my wife held the same principles instead of being so prejudiced it almost smacks of racialism.

SALLY: I am not prejudiced. I just think birds of a feather should stick together.

DAVID: But that is prejudice.

SALLY: No it's not... It makes no difference to me if a gay is black or white... It's just being gay makes them an unnatural species... Even the Bible agrees with that.

DAVID: That is open to interpretation.

SALLY: It's in black and white.

DAVID: But open to interpretation.

SALLY: Nonsense.

DAVID: *(Pauses to think)* What if I were to tell you I love Peter.

SALLY: *(Shocked)* What?

DAVID: See? That's your interpretation.

SALLY: *(Slowly)* You love him?

DAVID: Yes... Is that wrong?

SALLY: It's unnatural.

DAVID: But in the Bible it instructs me to do just that. "Love thy fellow man".

SALLY: Very clever I'm sure... So when can we expect him?

DAVID: I told him to get a taxi, but he said he preferred to walk... Are you not going to your bed?

SALLY: No. I think I'll keep up for a while.

DAVID: It would be better if we were alone, I think, for his sake.

SALLY: *(Mockingly)* Oh yes. Why's that then? Going to cry on your shoulder is he, while you stroke his hair and whisper sweet nothings into his ear? Ah, how sweet.

DAVID: Go to bed.

SALLY: No. If anyone wants to invite themselves here at gone midnight, then they'll have to take us, sorry, take you, as they find you, and that's married, with a wife, a female wife, and the possibility that she could be sitting in her own house and has every right to... And I want to meet this man you're always talking about.

DAVID: I am not always talking about him.

SALLY: Who else at the office do I know by name?

DAVID: I've worked with the man for twelve years, what can you expect? And I am not always talking about him. I may mention him from time to time, but that's only natural.

SALLY: Natural to talk about an unnatural?

DAVID: I hope when he arrives you're going to be a bit more sensitive... I don't want you embarrassing him with your prying questions.

SALLY: Come on, give me a bit of credit.

DAVID: I know what you are.

SALLY: Don't worry... I shan't let you down... I'll be the hostess to perfection... *(Thinks)* Perhaps we can discuss recipes... Or come to think of it, I wonder if he can help me with that sweater I'm knitting, I'm having one hell of a time getting that neck right.

The door bell rings.

DAVID: Good God, that can't possibly be him. Not this quick.

SALLY: Perhaps it's Jason.

DAVID: Jason has keys, remember?... My keys.

The door bell rings again.

SALLY: Well go and see who it is.

DAVID looks out of the window.

DAVID: Bloody hell... There's a police car outside.

SALLY: *(Alarmed)* Police?

DAVID: Jason. My car.

He exits to the front door.

WYATT: *(Off)* Good evening sir... Mr Jackson?

DAVID: *(Off)* Yes.

WYATT: *(Off)* May we come in sir?

DAVID: *(Off)* Yes. Yes. But has there been an accident..? Jason...?

WYATT: *(Off)* No sir. Just making enquiries.

They enter, DAVID first, followed by DETECTIVE INSPECTOR WYATT, who is dressed in plain clothes. Behind him is CONSTABLE PERKINS who is wearing uniform.

SALLY: Jason? Has he had an accident?

DAVID: No... Please sit down erm... erm...

WYATT: Wyatt. Detective Inspector Wyatt and this is Constable Perkins.

DAVID: How can we help you...? What's it about?

SALLY: Can I get you some tea or...? Please sit down.

PERKINS sits but WYATT remains standing. PERKINS jumps up onto his feet again.

WYATT: *(Indicates to Perkins to sit)* Rest your feet, Perkins. This could be a long night... *(To David)* Now sir. Mr. Jackson. Is that correct? Mr David Samuel Jackson?

DAVID: Yes... What's this all about?

WYATT: Have you been out this evening, sir?

DAVID: No... Yes.

WYATT: Well what is it sir? Yes or no?

DAVID: Yes... I went to the Chinese take-away.

WYATT: And at what time would this be sir?

DAVID: About half ten I think, I'm not sure.

WYATT: Did you go by car?

DAVID: No, I walked... It's only ten minutes down the road.

WYATT: And that's the only time you've been out tonight?

DAVID: Yes... Apart from coming home from work.

WYATT: And at what time would that be, sir?

DAVID: Five thirty. That's the time I got home... I left the office at five. Why? Why are you asking me all these questions?

WYATT: And did you drive home from work?

DAVID: Yes.

WYATT: Now Mr Jackson, are you the owner of a car registered CEX 529Y?

SALLY: It is Jason... He's had an accident.

WYATT: No, Mrs Jackson, no accident. Now sir, is this the registration number of your car?

DAVID: Yes... but...

WYATT: And where is the car now, sir?

DAVID: My son has it.

WYATT: Your son? This would be Jason, I gather?

DAVID: Yes.

WYATT: And where is he now, sir?

DAVID: I've no idea... You know what kids are like.

WYATT: Yes... Now... What time did Jason leave the house?

DAVID: Around ten.

WYATT: Did he say where he might be off to?

SALLY: He had a date with a girl.

WYATT: And the girl's name?

DAVID: We don't know... I was shocked to think he was meeting a girl at this time... I told him, when I was...

WYATT: *(Interrupting)* And he didn't say where he was meeting this girl or where he was taking her?

DAVID: No... Please, would you mind telling us what this is all about... Has he jumped a red light or something?

WYATT: And what time are you expecting him back?

DAVID: God knows... Kids today... What's he been up to?

WYATT: We'd just like to ask him a few questions.

SALLY: But what about?... Surely we have a right to know?

WYATT: I think you'd better sit down. *(They sit)* You said Jason was taking a girlfriend out this evening?

SALLY: Yes... But that's not a crime is it?

WYATT: But you don't know who the girl is?

SALLY: No.

WYATT: Or where he might be taking her?

SALLY: No.

WYATT: So your son stays out till the early hours, in your car, and you have no idea where he is or who he's with?

SALLY: He is twenty two.

DAVID: Actually, he didn't say he was meeting a girl.

SALLY: Of course he did.

WYATT: Who did he say he was meeting?

DAVID: He didn't say... Just that he was meeting someone.

SALLY: A girl!

DAVID: He didn't say a girl.

SALLY: What else would he go on a date with?

DAVID: And if you remember, he didn't actually say he was going on a date.

SALLY: Of course he did.

DAVID: No, you said it. He just said he was meeting someone.

WYATT: Such as mates?

DAVID: Possible... Please, won't you tell us what he's supposed to have done?

SALLY: He said he was going on a date with some girl.

DAVID: No he didn't.

WYATT: It's of no importance what he said... He could have been lying... Now think, are you certain you don't know of anywhere he might have gone?

DAVID: No... He just goes off night after night. Kids are like that.

WYATT turns away from them and takes a few slow steps turning slowly to face them as he speaks.

WYATT: Tell me... Is Jason a homosexual?

DAVID and SALLY react together.

DAVID: Good Lord, no.

SALLY: Certainly not.

WYATT turns away from them again.

WYATT: How often does Jason use your car, sir?

DAVID: Never as far as I'm concerned.

WYATT: But he has your car tonight?

DAVID: He took it without permission.

WYATT: I see... Does that often, does he?

DAVID: Yes, it has happened before.

WYATT: *(Turns back)* Tuesday of this week?

DAVID: No.

WYATT: You're certain of that?

DAVID: Certain... Now look I demand to know why you're so interested in the whereabouts of my car. It's fully insured, taxed and with a full MOT.

SALLY: God, all you can think about is that bloody car. What about Jason?

WYATT: We have reason to believe that your car was used this evening in a rather nasty piece of business.

DAVID: Nasty piece of business? Is that the way the police force talk nowadays?

WYATT: A witness gave us a description of your car sir and was perceptive enough to get the registration number as well. CEX 529Y. That is your car, is it not?

DAVID: Describe it.

WYATT: A grey Nissan Bluebird.

DAVID: Good Lord... What's he been up to?.. Please tell us... We'll do everything we can to help you... I'm sure there's been some sort of misunderstanding.

WYATT: At eleven ten this evening we received an anonymous phone call telling us a crime had been committed and the caller gave a description of your car as being involved.

SALLY: Anonymous? And you believed some crank who phoned you up with pie-in-the-sky information?

WYATT: What we found, Mrs Jackson, was not pie-in-the-sky.

SALLY: *(Stands. Speaks with anger)* For God's sake stop all this Columbo nonsense and spit it out... What is this anonymous caller accusing my son of?

WYATT: All reported incidents have to be followed up and, it may be as you say, just a crank, or, in this case, the guilty party, but we had to check it out.

SALLY: Check what out?

WYATT: A man almost beaten to death.*(SALLY and DAVID look at each other* *in shock. They know what is coming next)* So you see the first half of the pie-in-the-sky was indeed as reported... Now we have to check out the second half.

SALLY: Where did you find the man?

WYATT: Is it important?

DAVID: Was it Samson Lane woods?

WYATT: Yes sir. It was... Would you mind telling me how you knew that?

DAVID: Our daughter is a nurse in the casualty ward, she phoned and told us.

WYATT: Oh... And why should she do that?

DAVID: The man who was beaten is a friend of a friend of mine.

WYATT: A friend of a friend...?

SALLY: *(In panic)* He works with David.

WYATT: Who does?

SALLY: The friend of a friend.

WYATT: I'm sorry, but I'm lost here... *(To David)* Who did she say you work with?

SALLY: His lover. His wife. His boyfriend... *(She paces)* He's queer, isn't he? A queer... Queer bashing. Queer bashing, that's what this is, isn't it?.. A bloody queer gets bashed and you come here saying our Jason did it... Well he didn't... Let me tell you, he didn't... Some crank rings you up... gives you the first car number he sees and you come tearing around here while that crank is more than likely down there beating up another queer.

WYATT: *(Calmly)* And why should he do that?

SALLY: Do what?

WYATT: Ring us up?

SALLY: How the hell do I know...?

DAVID: If this caller was genuine, why didn't he help the guy who was beaten? And why didn't he give his name?

WYATT: Mrs Jackson, I think you should sit down.

SALLY: *(Sits)* This is a disgrace. Jason wouldn't do a thing like that.

WYATT: Now sir, in answer to your question, our informant this evening is in fact gay himself, of a sort. Recently he too had been a victim of these attackers himself. An attack that he did not report. He explained that he was afraid to... He's a married man, you see... But since he was attacked, he has been keeping watch on the cottage in Samson Lane. Intending revenge.

DAVID: Cottage? I didn't know there was a cottage down there?

SALLY: He means a gent's toilet!

DAVID: Eh?

WYATT: That's what they are called, sir, in the gay circles. Cottages.

DAVID: Not a real cottage? With roses around the door..?

WYATT: No sir... No roses around the door. A gentleman's toilet, as your wife pointed out.

DAVID: *(To Sally)* How did you know that?

SALLY: *(Obviously lying)* I read it some place.

WYATT: Can we go back to what you were saying about this man you work with sir?

DAVID: Peter... Peter Black...

WYATT: Ah yes... The other half... Would your son know his friend?

SALLY: Of course not.

WYATT: Sir?

DAVID: No... I just work with Peter... I've never met his friend, so I'm sure Jason wouldn't know either of them from Adam.

SALLY: And you think our Jason did this?

WYATT: We just want to ask him a few questions, that's all.

SALLY: But this is ridiculous.

WYATT: What is?

SALLY: Our son beating up a friend of my husband's friend... It's too much of a coincidence, wouldn't you say?

WYATT: Yes... Small world this, isn't it?

DAVID: So what's going to happen now?

WYATT: Well sir, if we'd caught young Jason tucked up in his bed we could have cleared up this matter tonight. For the moment, I'm going to leave Constable Perkins here to wait for Jason, with your permission of course. I, myself have other things to do... Find the anonymous caller for one.

DAVID: Why?

WYATT: *(Pauses. Speaks slowly)* He's threatened to kill the occupants of your car, sir.

SALLY: Oh God.

WYATT: Don't worry Mrs Jackson, maybe he's just what you said he was, a crank... And maybe the one who was responsible... Now if you'll excuse me. *(WYATT begins to leave)*

DAVID: What do we say to Jason when he arrives?

WYATT: Just tell him to co-operate... Goodnight to you both. *(Exits)*

SALLY: Oh my God.

DAVID: I'll kill him... I'll kill him.

WYATT enters.

WYATT: Perkins, move the car. If he sees it, he may do a runner.

PERKINS: Yes sir.

WYATT: Goodnight... See you later. *(Exits followed by PERKINS)*

SALLY: *(Walking around holding her head)* My mind, my mind, everything's so muddled... I can't think straight... Oh God... oh God.

DAVID: Sally, Sally, calm down... We have to keep a clear head about this... Jason didn't do this... I know he didn't... This caller obviously saw my car, took the number, went out and beat up Phillip and then reported it, saying my car was involved.

SALLY: But why should he do that?

DAVID: I have no idea, but... but... *(He stops abruptly. Turns to Sally with a look of horror. SALLY slowly removes her hands from her head and gives the same look of horror)*

SALLY: *(Slowly)* Oh my God.

DAVID: Peter.

SALLY: Will be here at any moment.

They both slowly look towards the door. SALLY lets out a loud gasp as her fingers go to her mouth.

The lights fade.

END OF ACT II

ACT III

Everything is as it was at the end of ACT II. SALLY and DAVID are in the same positions and they repeat the last three lines of that scene.

SALLY: *(Slowly)* Oh my God.

DAVID: Peter.

SALLY: Will be here at any moment.

They both look slowly towards the door. SALLY lets out a loud gasp as her fingers go to her mouth. They turn to look at one another. They remain silent.

DAVID: *(Eventually, almost a whisper)* What are we going to do?

SALLY: *(Whispering)* I don't know.

DAVID: *(Whispering)* I can't believe this is happening. I feel as though I'm in the middle of a Brian Rix farce.

SALLY: *(Whispering)* You'll have to go and meet him... Tell him it's not convenient.

DAVID: *(Loud)* Not convenient..?

SALLY: Shush.

DAVID: *(Whispering)* Why are we whispering?

SALLY: *(Whispering)* That policeman will be back any minute.

DAVID: But why are we whispering?

SALLY: *(Dropping the whisper)* We have to get rid of him.

DAVID: The policeman?

SALLY: No... Your gay friend.

DAVID: We can't just tell him to go...

SALLY: And you can't ask him in either... There'll be a copper here, remember.

DAVID: I'll take him for a walk...

SALLY: Walk...? Take him for a walk...? Good God... Aren't you forgetting something?

DAVID: What?

SALLY: Jason!

DAVID: Oh... Yes... Jason.

SALLY: Accused of beating a man nearly to death and you want to go walkies with his so-called lover?

DAVID: *(Long pause)* What if it's true?

SALLY: But it's not.

DAVID: But what if it is?

SALLY: *(Shouts)* But it's not... *(Turns away; softly)* How can you have any doubts?

DAVID: I don't know. I don't know... He was out on Tuesday night!

SALLY: So?

DAVID: That's when the other chap was attacked.

SALLY: *(Turning quickly)* And you think Jason was responsible?

DAVID: No... No.

SALLY: So what are you saying?

DAVID: I don't know.

SALLY: Well I do... I do... You think it was him, don't you? Your twisted mind is now turning over, full of twisted thoughts... Isn't it?... Now you know where he gets his money from, don't you?... Money for all his fancy leather jackets, don't you?... Of course, that's the answer... He goes out, picks up queers, beats their brains in just so he can go shopping the next day... Hasn't got a girlfriend... Perhaps a boyfriend, you're saying to yourself.

DAVID: I am thinking no such thing.

SALLY: Oh yes you are... I can hear you... Loud and clear, I can hear you.

DAVID: I refuse to be single-minded over this and... And...

SALLY: And? What?

DAVID: And... And doesn't it answer unanswered questions about our son?

SALLY: Such as?

DAVID: Where he gets his money from for one!

SALLY: Zak!

DAVID: Not one days work a week... He rolls in the stuff.

SALLY: Rolling in it? Is that why he wanted to borrow a fiver, because he's rolling in it?

DAVID: Out every night... till God knows when.

SALLY: Not every night.

DAVID: Well he's out now and he was out Tuesday night.

SALLY: You think he did it, don't you? You're convinced.

DAVID: Of course I don't want it to be him, but we have to face up to the possibility that it could be.

SALLY: You disgust me.

DAVID: *(Softly)* And if he did, how disgusted will you be then?

SALLY: *(Snaps)* If Jason is responsible, and I'm damned sure he's not, it could be because he's a man hater, because the one man he's supposed to love hates him... You.

DAVID: *(Moving quickly to her as though to strike)* Don't you ever repeat that... Never... Do you hear... I love my kids, and you damned well know it.

SALLY: *(Moves to kitchen exit)* Tell that to him. Not me. *(Exits)*

DAVID moves to kitchen exit. Stops abruptly. Turns, moves back into room. Looks at watch. Moves to window. Door bell rings. He exits)

SALLY enters, tense with worry. DAVID enters with CONSTABLE PERKINS. PERKINS appears nervous and uncomfortable.

DAVID: *(To Sally)* The policeman... To wait for Jason.

SALLY: Oh.

DAVID: Sit yourself down Constable... Constable...

PERKINS: Perkins, sir. Thank you. *(Sits on dining room chair)*

DAVID: Perhaps you'd be more comfortable here. *(Indicates an armchair)* Jason could be quite a while if his track record is anything to go by.

PERKINS: *(Stands)* Yes. *(Moves to David, speaks in a low voice)* Actually sir, I'd be a lot more comfortable if I could use your... your... *(Whispers)* toilet.

DAVID: Yes... yes. *(Points to kitchen exit)* Through there. Second on your right.

PERKINS: *(Moving to exit)* Thank you sir. Much appreciated. *(Exits)*

A silence.

SALLY: This will be cozy, won't it? Spending the night with a copper and your... friend... Are you going to tell him?

DAVID: Tell who?

SALLY: Perkins whatever?... Are you going to tell him who our next guest is?

DAVID: I suppose I'll have to... No... No... As I said, when Peter arrives, I'll suggest we go for a walk.

SALLY: And leave me here with P. C. Plod?

DAVID: What else can I do?

SALLY: And what if, while you're walking the streets with your... friend... Jason comes home?... No silly me, of course, your queer friends are more important than your family.

DAVID: That was uncalled for... But you're right... I'll just have to tell him to go.

SALLY: And will you tell him why?

DAVID: No... Of course not.

SALLY: Of course not.

DAVID: When all this mess is cleared up and we know for certain that Jason was not involved, I'll have to some way or another explain to Peter our position.

SALLY: I thought you were certain he was involved?

PERKINS enters.

PERKINS: Thanks. Much appreciated.

DAVID: Would you like a cup of tea?

PERKINS: I wouldn't say no.

DAVID: Fine. Sit yourself down and the wife'll make one.

SALLY: *(Softly)* Oh will she?

DAVID: *(Firmly)* Tea!

SALLY: *(Whispers)* You seem to have a thing about men that've just come out of the toilet.

DAVID: Tea! *(To Perkins)* Or would you prefer something stronger?

PERKINS: Tea would be fine.

SALLY exits. A Silence.

DAVID: *(Eventually)* This is a fine kettle of fish.

PERKINS: Yes sir.

DAVID: I just wish for once he'd get home at a decent hour so we can sort this mess out.

PERKINS: Yes sir.

DAVID: I suppose you're used to this sort of thing?

PERKINS: No sir. Not really.

DAVID: Oh, but I thought...?

PERKINS: I'm new to the city life. Spent most of my time as the village bobby, so to speak, sir. Moved down here three months ago. I needed the change, sir.

DAVID: Bright lights and all that, I suppose.

PERKINS: No, sir... Just a change.

DAVID: Funny sort of job yours, don't you think?

PERKINS: Yes sir.

DAVID: Never knowing what's around the next corner.

PERKINS: Like all jobs it has it's moments of boredom, sir.

DAVID: Please stop calling me sir.

PERKINS: City life's certainly less boring than the village, although even that had it's moments of excitement. There's always wrong un's in every community, however small. And weirdo's.

DAVID: Weirdo's?

PERKINS: Yes sir. Last thing I had to deal with, before I moved, was a local farmer having trouble with his new litter of pigs. Seems one morning he found one of them with a red cross drawn on it's back, for the rest of the day the piglet was most unwell.

DAVID: And he called the police?

PERKINS: No sir. The vet did.

DAVID: The vet?

PERKINS: Not straight away. You see, over the next few weeks, each one of the litter got marked with same cross, one at a time, so to speak, and every time the piglet was not quite itself for a while. The farmer thought someone was poisoning 'em. The vet, he knew better. He gave me a call, explained what he was suspicious of. Well sir, for the next few nights I had to conceal myself in the pig house. Not a very pleasant place to spend the night, I can tell you. Then, on the third night, in he came. A very respectable man, I can tell you. A business man who lived in the village... Well, in he comes, searching amongst the piglets, looking for one without a cross on it's back, and when he did, guess what?

DAVID: He put a cross on it's back?

PERKINS: More than that sir. Believe me or believe me not, he downed his trousers, sir, and had his end away.

DAVID: Good God... but why the cross?

PERKINS: He liked them to be virgins, sir.

DAVID: And you arrested him?

PERKINS: Of course.

DAVID: *(Laughing)* What did he say?... I mean, was he still... when you nabbed him?

PERKINS: Oh yes sir. Quite in a pitch of excitement he was when I put my hand on his shoulder. Dropped the piglet, pulled up his pants and begged me not to tell anyone. Tried to assure me that it wouldn't happen again. I'd caught him on his last conquest, so to speak... There were no more virgins left.

DAVID: Perhaps he thought the pigs squealed on him?

PERKINS: Very droll sir. But before you rack your brains for more gems like that one, I've heard them all. A village public house is full of comedians.

DAVID: What happened next?

PERKINS: I moved here sir and was attached to the vice-squad.

DAVID: Vice-squad? *(Struggles to say the next line)* Is that what that Wyatt was? A vice officer?

PERKINS: Yes sir.

DAVID: But why is he dealing with this?

PERKINS: The activity that goes on down at Samson Wood comes under our department.

DAVID: Because of the toilet?

PERKINS: Yes sir. It's called a cottage... An insult to the name... Where I come from a cottage is something to be proud of... A thing of beauty.

DAVID: Yes. Roses around the door. *(Stands)* Like this one. *(Indicates puzzle)*

PERKINS stands, looks at the puzzle.

PERKINS: Yes sir, exactly.

SALLY enters with a tray containing cups of tea.

DAVID: Ah, tea up.

SALLY gives David a fierce look as he and Perkins sit down.

SALLY: Do you take sugar P.C. Whatever?

PERKINS: Perkins mam. Three.

SALLY: Three?

PERKINS: Yes, if you don't mind.

SALLY: No, I'll go and get the sugar bowl. *(Exits)*

PERKINS: Little woman seems a bit tense.

DAVID: Yes, well under the circumstances.

PERKINS: Yes, suppose so.

SALLY enters with sugar bowl, puts two spoonfuls into Perkins cup with shaking hand, misses cup with third spoonful, drops sugar bowl onto tray, quickly turns away.

SALLY: Oh God... oh God.

DAVID stands, puts arm around her.

DAVID: Perhaps you'd be better if you went and had a lie down.

She shrugs him off.

SALLY: I'm all right... I'm fine. *(Turns sharply to Perkins)* Are you going to be here long?

PERKINS: That depends.

SALLY: On what?

PERKINS: On how long your son takes to show up.

SALLY: Don't you have to have a warrant for this sort of thing?

PERKINS: What sort of thing is that?

SALLY: Taking up residence in innocent people's homes?

PERKINS: It is in your interests and Inspector Wyatt did ask your permission.

SALLY: In our interests?

PERKINS: In Jason's interests.

SALLY: But he didn't do this.

PERKINS: Well then as soon as he comes home the sooner we can clear it all way, so to speak.

SALLY: Trouble is with you coppers, once you get a bee in your bonnet, there's no getting it out... You think our Jason did it and there'll be no telling you different.

DAVID: I think you'd better lay down before you say something you'll regret.

SALLY: I'm in my own house and I'll say what ever I like. *(Turns on Perkins)* Tell me, do you get pleasure out of this?

PERKINS: Out of what?

SALLY: Hounding people... setting up house, filling their heads with God knows how many worries... My Jason didn't do this... He couldn't... He wouldn't... It's not in his nature... He's a good boy... You have no right... No right... I don't want you in my house.

PERKINS: I'm sorry Mrs Jackson... but I'm only doing my job... I'll try not to be a nuisance, but it is in Jason's interests.

SALLY: Sod Jason's interests.

DAVID: Calm down.

SALLY: Have you told him? Have you..?

DAVID: Not yet.

SALLY: Well tell him. *(Moves to exit)* Tell him. *(Exits)*

DAVID: She's upset.

PERKINS: Understandable.

DAVID: I just wish he'd come home.

PERKINS: Just the one?

DAVID: No. We have a girl, too. Jenny. She's older than Jason. Twenty six. She's a nurse.

PERKINS: Ah, yes, I remember you told Inspector Wyatt.

DAVID: It's at times like these you wish you'd never had kids. Nothing but worry.

PERKINS: Lot of trouble is he?

DAVID: Jason? No, not really. He's unemployed. You married?

PERKINS: Yes.

DAVID: Children?

PERKINS: Yes. Seven.

DAVID: Seven?

PERKINS: We wanted a girl you see.

DAVID: Seven boys?

PERKINS: Afraid so... Better luck next time.

DAVID: I'd give up if I were you old son.

PERKINS: Too late for that, she's with child again. Six months gone.

DAVID: Glutton for punishment, aren't you?

PERKINS: Just a bit... You're supposed to be telling me something?

DAVID: Eh?

PERKINS: Your wife said you were...

DAVID: Oh, yes.... Difficult... An unbelievable situation, really.

PERKINS: Try me. After the piggy poker I'll believe anything.

DAVID: *(Paces)* This chap who's down the hospital, well, as we said, his friend is a friend of mine, and Jenny, that's my daughter, as I told you is a nurse, she phoned me to tell me about this friend of my friend and that my friend was down there and his friend's parents had arrived and the father of my friend's friend was giving him a hard time and could I help out in any way. So I spoke to him on the phone, my friend that is, not my friend's friend's father, and he was most upset. Well you can understand why, can't you? I asked him to come here and wait and if there's anything he should know about his friend then Jenny would ring. So you see, he's on his way here now and God knows what he's going to think when he finds you here. What am I going to tell him...?

PERKINS: *(Scratches his head)* Well, if you don't mind me saying so, why not tell him what you just told me, that should keep him guessing for an hour or more.

DAVID: Did I confuse you?

PERKINS: Just a bit... Now let's see if I can work it out. You have this friend?

DAVID: Yes... Peter Black.

PERKINS: Ah. The other half, so to speak?

DAVID: Yes.

PERKINS: And his friend is not a friend of yours?

DAVID: No.

PERKINS: But your friend's friend knows you're his friend's friend?

DAVID: I don't think so, why?

PERKINS: How friendly?

DAVID: How friendly what?

PERKINS: How friendly are you with his friend...? *(Winks)* You know... Takes all sorts.

DAVID: *(Shocked)* He works with me... Good God... I'm married.

PERKINS: So was the man who fell in love with pork chops, sir.

DAVID: Now look here, Peter is just a work colleague. Nothing more.

PERKINS: That you've invited to your house at this hour?

DAVID: Yes. That's what friends are for. He's upset. What else could I do? What would you have done?

PERKINS: It wouldn't arise sir, if you don't mind me saying so. I wouldn't have friends who were that way inclined.

DAVID: My God, you sound just like my wife.

PERKINS: How's that sir?

DAVID: Prejudiced.

PERKINS: If you say so, sir. I always say every man has the right to his opinions. Not so long ago, thirty years back, it was against the law just to be that way, and rightly so, in my opinion. Law should never have been changed. While they're locked away they can't go out contaminating others. Law should never have been changed.

DAVID: It's not a disease you contaminate others with.

PERKINS: Isn't it...?

DAVID: Of course not.

PERKINS: So how come they learn to do it if nobody shows them how?

DAVID: It's natural.

PERKINS: Is it? I was always led to believe it was unnatural. But then you're entitled to your opinion.

DAVID: Fat lot of help you're going to be when he arrives.

PERKINS: If it's all the same to you, I'd rather not be of any help, thank you very much.

DAVID: Couldn't you go and sit in your car or something?

PERKINS: I have to stay here.

DAVID: Look, when he arrives, I'm going to suggest to him that we go for a walk.

PERKINS: In the rain, sir?

DAVID: Yes in the rain, if need be.

PERKINS: I could always sit in the kitchen with your good lady.

DAVID: *(Slaps hand over face)* Good God, this is a Brian Rix.

PERKINS: A Brian Rix, sir?

DAVID: Oh never mind... Look, I want you to try and understand the predicament I'm in.

PERKINS: I'll try, sir.

DAVID: *(With despair)* Will you please stop calling me sir.

PERKINS: I'll try.

DAVID: Any moment now the door bell will ring and standing on my doorstep will be a man, a most upset man, looking for the comfort of friendship, but little does he know that the possible reason for his distress was caused by my son. Now, you appreciate that it puts me in a most delicate position. I have to employ all of my tact to break it to him as gently as I possibly can and it would be cruel, to say the least, for him to walk in here and hear it from your unsympathetic mouth. Do you understand?

PERKINS: I think so sir.

DAVID: I'll call the wife and you and she can sit in the kitchen and discuss all of your opinions and prejudices, you have a lot in common. You'll get on like a house on fire.

PERKINS: If you say so, sir.

DAVID moves to the stairs exit.

DAVID: *(Calling)* Sally... Sally. Are you asleep?

SALLY: *(Off)* No.

DAVID: Can you come down for a moment?

SALLY: *(Off)* Why?

DAVID: Come down and I'll tell you.

PERKINS: Seems a pity to disturb the lady.

DAVID: She's already disturbed. We're all disturbed at the moment. These are very disturbing times.

SALLY enters.

SALLY: What do you want?

DAVID: Me and Perkins here have come up with a solution.

SALLY: What solution? Solution to what?

DAVID: When Peter arrives, Perkins is going to sit in the kitchen until I've explained things.

SALLY: Oh. *(Turns)* I'm now going back to my bed.

DAVID: No. I want you in the kitchen with Perkins.

SALLY: Why?

DAVID: To act as liaison officer.

SALLY: Liaison officer?

DAVID: Yes. Look, I can't have Perkins here getting restless and wandering in.

SALLY: Why not?

DAVID: Sit and have a chat with him in the kitchen for ten minutes or so and you'll begin to understand why. You and him have a lot in common. You'll enjoy it. Perhaps between the two of you, you could organise a community group that'll dress up in white sheets with pointed hoods over their heads with the intention of scouring the neighbourhood looking for individuals that don't quite come up to the required approval and can be educated as to the error of their ways. Such as hanging them from the nearest tree or tying them to a burning cross.

SALLY: *(To Perkins)* Has he been drinking?

PERKINS: Not that I know of, Mam, but I have to say he has some very strange ideas does your husband. Very strange.

SALLY: And he exaggerates.

PERKINS: Yes...

SALLY: All the time.

PERKINS: Yes...

DAVID: I do not.

SALLY: All the time... He does it to brighten up his dull life. But then lots of men do that... Because of their job usually... Pen pushing... I expect your job is full of excitement... I bet your life's not dull.

PERKINS: Indeed not.

SALLY: And when you get home I expect everyday you have something different to tell your wife? Not like him... Same old subject... Day after day... *(To David)* Now if you'd been a policeman like our Constable Perkins here...

DAVID: *(Interrupting)* But I'm not a policeman, I'm a tax inspector, and tax inspectors talk about taxes, and as for our Constable Perkins, our Mr Wonderful, from what I gather he has only one thing to say to his wife when he walks through the door and that's, "Get 'em off"!

PERKINS: What he means, mam, is I've got seven kids.

SALLY: Seven!

PERKINS: All boys.

SALLY: My, my.

PERKINS: And another on the way.

SALLY: My goodness. *(Takes his arm)* I think we will go into the kitchen, Constable. I'll make you more tea. No wonder you need three sugars, burning up all that energy. My, haven't you got muscular arms? *(Squeezes his biceps, looks at David)* All man. I like a man to have muscles in his arms. Better than muscles in the head. *(They move to kitchen exit)*

PERKINS: I like to keep myself in shape, so to speak.

SALLY: *(Still looking at David)* Oh yes I can see you do. Seven sons? My, my.

DAVID: Make sure you keep a look out for Jason.

SALLY: Do you have photos?

DAVID: I said, keep a look out for Jason.

PERKINS: One or two. In my wallet.

DAVID: Did you hear what I said?

PERKINS: What's that, sir?

DAVID: Keep a look out for Jason.

PERKINS: Oh have no fear of that, sir.

DAVID: My fear is you'll be so engrossed talking about yourself and drinking tea that he could walk in, cook himself a meal, eat it, and you wouldn't even notice.

PERKINS: Oh no, sir. I always could do several things at once.

SALLY: And of course Constable Perkins will notice him. Who do you think he is? His father?

DAVID: No, just an over-sexed bullock.

PERKINS: No need for that kind of talk Mr Jackson, especially in front of your good woman.

SALLY: No, no need indeed.

DAVID: And where are you going?

SALLY: Into the kitchen.

DAVID: Why?

SALLY: Because you said.

DAVID: When Peter arrives.

SALLY: Oh... But I was going to make more tea.

DAVID: *(Turning away)* Tea! Tea! We shouldn't be sitting around drinking tea. This thing is such a nightmare that we all seem to be forgetting what it's all about. Any moment now my son could walk through that door and as soon as he does, will be marched down to the cop shop and be arrested for a brutal crime.

SALLY: Arrested? Don't be silly. *(To Perkins)* Arrest him?

PERKINS: 'Fraid so, mam.

SALLY: Arrest him? But why...? He didn't do this... Believe me, he didn't.

PERKINS: *(Moving back to chair)* For his sake, I hope you're right. *(Sits)* Pretty nasty business all round. *(Pause. Looks at David)* Some might say not. All I know is, it's against the law to smash someone's head in, and *(Pause)* it's my job to uphold the law. *(Pause)* Without prejudice, so to speak. Regardless of who's head it might be.

SALLY: *(Softly)* He didn't do it... Arrested?

PERKINS: Now don't you worry... If he didn't do it he'll have every opportunity to clear himself down at the station.

DAVID: And we all know what that means.

PERKINS: I'm sorry sir, I don't quite catch your drift.

DAVID: *(Moves to table)* Like a puzzle. *(Picks up a piece)* Just like a puzzle. Bits and pieces. Something happens down in the darkness of Samson Wood. A picture is painted then cut up into tiny pieces without anyone but the artist seeing the canvas... A pretty ugly picture.

PERKINS: Are you feeling unwell, sir?

DAVID: *(Moves angrily to Perkins, thrusts piece to his face)* Just like this. Just like this. Evidence. Fragmented evidence, and you, you and your tribe will put that picture together no matter what, even if the pieces don't quite fit, you'll twist and bend them. *(Twists piece)* Until they do. And if this knobbly bit don't fit, well, tear it off. *(Rips off round bit of piece)* Then it'll fit. Yes. Then it'll fit. *(Turns, moves away)*

PERKINS: *(Slowly)* All leads have to be investigated, sir. *(Picks up destroyed piece)* Picture will have a hole in it now, sir. *(Looks at piece)* Roses. Be a couple of roses short... pity... Such a pity... And sir... may I remind you the one piece of the picture that we do have is oblong in shape... and rather large... A grey Nissan Bluebird... So large we can see the registration number plate.... Sir.

SALLY: *(Loud protest)* Given to you by some other pervert. My God... I could walk out this very minute, take down any car number, ring the police and say I saw it down there.

PERKINS: But you didn't... And do you know why you didn't?

SALLY: But I could have!

PERKINS: Because you had no reason to do so... Also we have a description of the driver.

DAVID: *(Softly)* A description?

PERKINS: Yes sir.

SALLY: *(Moves around room in nervous tension)* But why would this caller do that? Why would he calmly sit and watch this obscene thing happen and not do anything...? I don't understand it... I don't.

PERKINS: There were three of them, mam... Take a brave man to tackle three men, mam.

SALLY: But he left him there... After.... Isn't that what the Inspector said?

PERKINS: Yes he did.

SALLY: But why?

PERKINS: That's something we still have to figure out.

SALLY: He's obviously responsible.

PERKINS: Maybe... but then why ring us at all... Another mystery, so to speak.

DAVID: *(Turns sharply)* Couldn't it be possible that he didn't mean to hurt him?

PERKINS: How's that, sir?

DAVID: Let's paint a new picture... A man down on his luck... Perhaps not eaten for a day or two... Reads in the paper, like we did tonight, about a man being robbed down Samson Woods... Let's say this man knew what went on down there and thought... Easy... Pick up a guy... Take him to the woods... Lure him there... You know... Offer you know what, but, intending to rob him... But perhaps it didn't work according to plan... Perhaps the guy put up a fight and with his desperate need, brought on by hunger, he hit the man too hard... Perhaps lost control... And after was so filled with guilt he phoned the police to make sure the guy didn't bleed to death or something... See you never thought of that, did you?... You police, you make me laugh... No imagination.

PERKINS: Oh but sir, we did think of that possibility, but you seem to be forgetting one thing, sir.

DAVID: And what's that, that the police have brains? Forgive me, but that's so easy to forget.

PERKINS: Assumption.

DAVID: Assumption?

PERKINS: Your explanation is based on assumption... Also this is the ninth attack in two years, sir, that have been reported... Plus unreported attacks... such as our informant this evening.

SALLY: He could have been lying.

PERKINS: Oh yes, he could. But he gave us information, true or false, that we have to follow up, especially this one. Inspector Wyatt, who's been doing this sort of thing since the year dot, told me it was the worst case of beating that he's ever been involved with. "Lucky to be alive", he said. "Couldn't possibly be the work of one man"... so we have to follow up any leads... I'm sure you understand.

DAVID: But...

PERKINS: And when young Jason arrives all he has to do is convince us differently.

SALLY: You said this bloke gave a description of the driver?

PERKINS: Yes, mam... A rough description... It was dark he said.

DAVID: But not too dark to read a registration plate.

PERKINS: The car was left on the road.

SALLY: So what did he say the driver looked like?

PERKINS: I'm afraid I can't tell you that.

DAVID: Why not...? You think when Jason comes in I'm going to rush and give him cosmetic surgery in the hall?

PERKINS: Dark hair?

SALLY: Millions have dark hair.

PERKINS: Leather jacket?

DAVID and SALLY look at each other. SALLY turns away.

SALLY: How many leather jackets are there in the world?

PERKINS: Blue faded jeans and white trainer shoes.

SALLY: *(In panic)* But that's a description of almost half the young men in this town.

PERKINS: Driving a grey Nissan Bluebird, registration number...

DAVID: *(Interrupting)* Yes, yes, we know all that.

PERKINS: So you see we do have to follow up all...

DAVID: Yes... Yes...

The doorbell rings.

SALLY: Oh God... I'm about to lose my mind. *(Becomes hysterical)* It's him... Get rid of him... Get rid of him David... David... David... Get.. Get... Him...

DAVID moves to her, takes her in his arms. She bursts into loud sobbing.

DAVID: Sally. Sally.

SALLY: I don't want him here... I don't want him here. *(She pulls away from him. She gets a firm grip of herself. Wipes her eyes. Speaks very directly)* Understand this David, I want you to get rid of him. I don't know how you're going to do it. But get rid of him. *(Exits to the kitchen)*

Doorbell rings.

PERKINS: Want me to tell him to go away, sir?

DAVID: No I do not.

PERKINS: Little woman don't want him here, sir.

DAVID: But I do.

PERKINS: Yes, so you said... Well sir... Takes all sorts...Think I'll go and comfort your little woman, if it's all the same to you.

DAVID: Yes. You do that.

PERKINS: *(Moves to kitchen exit)* If she makes more tea, sir, would you like me to bring it through?

DAVID: Certainly not... Tell my wife to do it.

PERKINS: Don't think she'd like that sir.

DAVID: Just go will you.

Doorbell rings.

PERKINS: Better get rid of him before...

DAVID: Yes I know... Please... Go drink tea or something.

PERKINS exits. DAVID moves to the hall entrance. Exits.

DAVID: *(Off)* Sorry about that Peter... I was through the back... Come in... Come in... God what a night.

He enters followed by PETER BLACK. PETER is a good-looking man in his forties. He is dressed in a sober suit and tie. None of his characteristics would give away his homosexuality. He is obviously distressed given the situation, but maintains the manly trait of withholding his emotions to the best of his abilities.

PETER: This really is good of you, David... I honestly feel I shouldn't be here, but...

DAVID: Nonsense.

PETER: Nice room.

DAVID: Yes... Sit yourself down.

PETER: Thank you.

DAVID: My wife's busy in the kitchen... Would you like a cup of tea...? Or what about a scotch?

PETER: Scotch... If you don't mind.

DAVID: No, course not. *(Goes to sideboard, pours out two scotches)* Nasty night. Went out earlier to get a Chinese... Got soaked... Like something with it?

PETER: Straight, thanks.

DAVID moves over to him with the drinks. PETER is leaning forwards, staring at his shoes.

DAVID: Cheerio.

DAVID takes a drink.

PETER: Cheerio. *(Downs drink in one)* God. Needed that.

DAVID: Another?

PETER: Better not.

A silence. DAVID sits opposite.

DAVID: Nasty business.

PETER: *(Softly)* Yes... Very nasty.

DAVID: How is he?

PETER: I don't know... Only what Jenny told me... I think she was just being kind... Keeping the worst from me.

DAVID: Didn't they let you...?

PETER: See him? No... His parents were there... Relatives only... They made sure of that... His mother's okay... His father has never really accepted the idea.

DAVID: I see.

PETER: I understand how he feels... I mean how many fathers would want their only son living with another man? Living as... You know.

DAVID: He sounds a pretty unreasonable character to me.

PETER: No... Just a father... Like all fathers... Like you.

DAVID: I'm sure, given the circumstances, I...

PETER: Would have slapped me on the back and wished us all the happiness in the world? You're a father, David, and, however tolerant you might think you are, when it comes to your own there's always disappointment.

DAVID: But given the circumstances...

PETER: When a man realises he's gay, one of the first things he has to live with is the disappointment of his parents... However much they say they love you and that it doesn't make a scrap of difference, they can't hide their disappointment... It's there, all the time, in their eyes.

DAVID: How bad did Jenny say he was?

PETER: Fractured skull... Broken ribs... Punctured lung... Lost a great deal of blood... God, the bastards...

DAVID: *(Stands. Moves around)* Did the police see you?

PETER: Yes.

DAVID: Did they give any hope of catching..?

PETER: Yes... They have a description...

DAVID: Oh... Did they treat you badly?

PETER: No. They were quite sympathetic, understanding really. You hear stories about the police, but as far as I'm concerned, they've enough sense to realise their job is difficult enough without complicating it with personal prejudices.

DAVID: *(Looking to kitchen)* Not everyone would agree with that... *(Pauses)* So they told you everything?

PETER: As much as they wanted me to know, I suppose... They had a telephone call... A witness. He gave a description of the men and the car they were driving.

DAVID: Haven't you wondered who this man might have been? This witness? Could it have been him who did it?

PETER: Why should he phone the police?

DAVID: I don't know. Seems strange him seeing what happened and then disappearing.

PETER: How do you know he disappeared?

DAVID: *(Quickly)* Jenny said.

PETER: How did she know?

DAVID: Police told her I expect... Or perhaps she overheard.

PETER: Oh... Yes, possible... There's only curtains dividing down at the casualty... But whoever he was, Phillip owe's his life to him. Without that call he would have been a dead man.

A silence.

DAVID: *(Sudden courage)* Did you know he was down there?

PETER: *(Hangs his head)* No, I didn't.

DAVID: Did you know he goes there?

PETER: No... No...

DAVID: But he knew what goes on in Samson Woods?

PETER: Yes... So do I... But I don't go there... I had no reason to... Years ago, yes, but not since Phillip and I... You know...

DAVID: So you both know the dangers of Samson Woods?

PETER: Of course... That's where I met him... Every gay around here knows about Samson Woods.

DAVID: So why do they go there?

PETER: Loneliness I suppose.

DAVID: But it's dangerous.

PETER: Sometimes you can be so alone the only person you feel you have to fear is yourself. It's not so bad nowadays, but not so long back, being gay, and being alone with it, was like being addicted to a drug, you crave it, you have to have it. Sex, yes, but not just sex. Just to be with someone as lonely as yourself, if only for an hour. Two lonely people have something very special to give to each other... Hope.

SALLY enters. She carries a tray holding coffee cups and a coffee pot.

SALLY: I thought you might like coffee.

DAVID: Ah... Sally, this is Peter. I don't think you two have met.

PETER stands. Holds out his hand.

PETER: How do you do, Mrs Jackson.

SALLY shakes his hand. She does not smile.

SALLY: How do you do.

PETER: Well...

SALLY: Yes...

PETER: You have a nice home.

SALLY: Thank you.

PETER: I feel as though I already know you.

SALLY: How's that?

PETER: David talks about you non-stop at the office.

SALLY: You surprise me.

DAVID: *(To Sally)* Have you finished in the...?

SALLY: Have you, you know what?

DAVID: No... Of course not.

PETER frowns, not understanding their conversation.

SALLY: Are you going to?

DAVID: Yes... Aren't you worrying something might be burning in the kitchen?

SALLY: *(Sits)* No... Just go and check dear... I'll keep Peter amused for a minute or two.

DAVID: Peter's not in the mood to be amused.

PETER: Actually, yes I am. The one thing I could do with right now is a good laugh.

DAVID: *(Turns his back to Peter, gives Sally a "Good God, what are we going* *to do?" look)* So... 'Em... What's... What's cooking in the kitchen?

SALLY: Fairy cakes. *(David scowls)* Go and check them for me dear... I know how *you* hate fairies with burnt wings.

PETER laughs. DAVID scowls again and exits.

PETER: He's far too sensitive.

SALLY: Yes... You didn't mind?

PETER: No, of course not.

SALLY: You're not at all what I expected, you know.

PETER: No, I don't suppose I am.

SALLY: It's like talking to someone on the telephone, they never look the way you imagined them to look.

PETER: No, very true... I expect you were expecting pink tights, frilly blouse, mascara... A little touch of rouge on the cheeks...?

SALLY: *(Smiles)* Well not that extreme.

PETER: Sorry to disappoint you.

SALLY: Pay no mind to me. You've been discussed so many times over my dining table, I really didn't know what to expect... And I'm not disappointed... Actually, I'm quite pleasantly surprised... Looking at you, I'm wondering why you haven't been hounded by women... You don't look...

PETER: Gay?

SALLY: You just don't look....

PETER: Gay?

SALLY: Is your friend..?

PETER: Gay?

SALLY: No. I know he's... Well he must be... What I meant is... Is he...?

PETER: Camp?

SALLY: Yes.

PETER: Just a bit.

SALLY: So he's the female of the two?

PETER: *(Bursts into laughter)* Mrs Jackson...

SALLY: Call me Sally.

PETER: Sally... Phillip is a man... Not female...

SALLY: I thought that one was... You know... The man... and the other...

PETER: I'm sorry to disappoint you once again but there's nothing female about Phillip. He doesn't flit about the house in a pink negligee dusting with a feather duster, nor does he spend hours in the kitchen over a hot stove... No fairy cakes from Phillip... I do all the cooking and domestic chores... Phillip's either sitting in front of the tele watching football, or he's out in the yard stripping his motorbike down... *(Turns from her. Sombre)* ... And now... And now he's fighting for his life.

A silence.

SALLY: Are you angry?

PETER: Angry?

SALLY: At whoever it was that did it?

PETER: At the moment I haven't time for anger... All I want is for Phillip to get over this... Without complications.

SALLY: Complications?

PETER: They've fractured his skull. He's lost a great deal of blood... Could leave him brain damaged.

SALLY: They told you that?

PETER: No... But I'm intelligent enough to face up to facts.

SALLY: So you're not angry?

PETER: No... Just worried.

SALLY: What would you do if one of... Phillip's... attackers.. walked through that door right now?

PETER: That's hypothetical...

SALLY: Assume they did.

PETER: I don't know.

SALLY: Would you be angry?

PETER: No... I honestly don't think I would be.

SALLY: Why not?

PETER: Because I'm angry with Phillip.

SALLY: Why?

PETER: For going to that bloody place... My God, what was he thinking of...? He know's the risks.

SALLY: So you think he got what he deserves?

PETER: Of course not... I suppose you think he did?

SALLY: A fool plays with lions. A fool gets scratched.

PETER: Much more than a scratch, I can assure you.

SALLY stands, turns away.

SALLY: How are Phillip's parents taking all this?

PETER: Same as me... Worried sick.

SALLY: Do they love him?

PETER: Of course.

SALLY: But they don't love the idea that he's what he is... Gay?

PETER: No, not really...

SALLY: And what about your parents?

PETER: Something I never had to worry about... I was brought up in an institution... An orphan.

SALLY: I see... Is that why you're...?

PETER: Gay?

SALLY: Yes.

PETER: Perhaps... It goes on... Institutions, orphanages, boarding schools... Well known fact...

SALLY: So if you had parents, would you expect them to be supportive?

PETER: Of course.

SALLY: So you believe parents should stand by their children no matter what?

PETER: Depends... If I were lucky enough to be a father, the one quality I would seek, would be the quality of understanding.

SALLY: Ah. *(Turns but does not look at him)* At this very precise moment I am in a situation that I am finding very difficult to handle. A situation concerning my son. I love my son. I trust my son. And, until this evening, I believed I understood him and had no reason to question that understanding... But now, because of you, because of your... whatever you care to call him... my head is like a courtroom. Judge and jury... for and against... questioning my understanding of my son.

PETER: I'm sorry but I can't quite make out what you're trying to tell me.

SALLY: *(Looks at him)* Out there *(points to kitchen)* sitting at my kitchen table is another uninvited guest... a policeman... And have you any idea what he's doing there?

PETER: I'm afraid I...

SALLY: And if, and when you do find out why he's there, will you even spare one second to try and understand?

PETER: Understand what?

SALLY: The policeman is waiting for my son... Jason... Waiting to question him... Accusing him... Wrongly accusing him of...

DAVID has entered during her lines.

DAVID: Sally shut up... Leave this to me.

SALLY: *(Loud)* Accusing him of queer bashing.

DAVID: *(Grabbing her)* Sally.

SALLY: *(Screams)* Queer bashing your queer.

DAVID: *(Pushes her into chair)* You stupid woman. *(Turns to Peter who stands very still in shock provoked thought)* Peter... Peter, we have to talk... This is all some silly misunderstanding.

PETER: *(Softly)* Your son... Jason....

SALLY: *(With venom)* Don't you dare mention his name... You're not fit to mention his name.

DAVID: Sally, for God's sake.

SALLY: I will not have filth like him mentioning his name. *(PETER keeping* *very calm moves slightly towards her)*

PETER: Filth?... Filth?... Filth like me?... What kind of filth is Jason, eh?... Jason and his friends...?

SALLY: And what kind of filth was your friend seeking...? As far as I'm concerned, he got exactly what he deserved.

DAVID: Shut up will you... For God's sake.

PETER: I think I'd better leave.

DAVID: Peter, I want you to know...

PERKINS enters.

PERKINS: Is everything all right, Mrs Jackson?

DAVID: Oh God.

PERKINS: No trouble I hope? *(Looks at Peter)* Good evening sir... *(PETER glares at him)* Not been upsetting the little lady, I hope?

PETER: I think I can safely leave that to you.

PERKINS: Oh, how's that sir?

Telephone rings.

PETER: Jesus. *(Moves to exit)*

DAVID: Peter hang on, this could be Jenny. *(Picks up receiver)* Hello... Yes he is... Hold on. *(To Perkins)* It's for you.

PERKINS: *(Takes receiver)* Hello, Perkins here.

PETER moves to exit. DAVID grabs him.

DAVID: Please Peter... Can't we talk this over... It's all a misunderstanding... I'm sure of it.

PERKINS: Yes, sir... I understand, sir... He's here, sir... Yes, sir... *(To Peter)* Hold hard, sir... something you should know about. *(Into receiver)* Yes, sir... No, sir... No trouble... Goodbye, sir. *(Replaces receiver)* I think you should all sit down. *(To Peter)* Especially you, sir.

PETER: I'm leaving.

PERKINS: No, sir... Not yet.

DAVID sits next to SALLY. PETER remains standing. PERKINS moves to face Sally and David.

DAVID: What is it?

PERKINS: *(Slowly)* Another phone call, sir... Same man... Told us where we can find your car, sir.

DAVID: Where?

PERKINS: Far end of Samson Woods, sir... Inspector Wyatt is on his way now, sir, checking it out.

DAVID: What about Jason?

PERKINS: Didn't say, sir.

DAVID: Did he say if the car was all right?

PERKINS: Didn't say, sir. Inspector Wyatt is going to ring back with any news. *(Pause)* And I'm afraid the next thing I have to say is not so good, so to speak. *(Pause)* No, sir, not good at all. *(Looks at Peter, lowers eyes)* I'm sorry, sir.

SALLY: Sorry...? *(Looks at Peter who is standing expressionless as though understanding. Looks back at Perkins, stands, moves towards him raising voice slightly)* Sorry for what?

PERKINS: I'm afraid... I'm afraid the young man... The young man... They lost him... so to speak.

DAVID: *(Softly with shock)* Lost him?

PERKINS: Yes, sir. *(To Peter)* I'm afraid your... friend... passed away, sir, in the operating theatre.

PETER: *(Whispers)* No.

PERKINS: I'm afraid so.

PETER: No... no...

DAVID: Oh God.

PETER: *(Softly)* God? Is there such a person?

DAVID: Peter, I'm so sorry.

PETER: To take a life... such a young life... an innocent life.... For what reason?.. And in such a way?

DAVID: I think we'd better get you to the hospital.

PETER: *(Raising his voice slightly)* No. I want nothing from you. Nothing. *(To Perkins)* But I want something from you. *(Loud)* Find him. Find him. Find their murdering son. Find him before I do.

SALLY: *(Sharply)* My son is innocent.

PETER: *(With venom to Perkins)* Find him.

SALLY: Jason didn't do this... Get that through your head will you. My son is not involved.

PETER: *(To Sally)* Well I think differently. *(Points at Perkins)* And so does he... Your son, madam, killed the only thing that was of any value in my life.

SALLY: *(Loud)* Value? Value?

DAVID: Shut up, Sally.

SALLY: No, I won't shut up. Oh I know you'll be on his side. Never mind about your son... Just as long as you keep on the right side of your poncy friends. *(Turns on Peter)* And what value did he put on you when he went out cruising around the woods..? Popping in and out of the cottage like a demented Jack-in-the-box..? What value were you to him then?

PETER: You are sick.

DAVID: Sally, will you keep it shut.

SALLY: Me sick..? Me sick..? I suppose you think what your little friend was doing was healthy? It's perverted. Perverted. And if you ask me he got just what he deserved.

PETER: *(Angry. To Perkins)* Tell her... Tell her.

PERKINS: Tell her what?

PETER: Everything.

PERKINS: Sorry, sir, I don't really know what...?

PETER: *(Turning on Sally)* Pervert..? Pervert...? Because I'm homosexual you class me as perverted. Well, Mrs Jackson, just how do you see your dear, dear son?

DAVID: Peter.. Please...

SALLY: Get him out of my house... Get him out.

PETER: Have no fear, I'm going. I don't want to be here when your filth arrives. I may not be responsible for what I might do. *(He moves to exit)*

SALLY: *(Almost screaming)* Filth..? Filth...? At least he wouldn't indulge in the filth you practice.

PETER: *(Turns in fury)* Shut up. Shut your stupid, evil, venomous mouth! For your information, and you're soon to find out, Phillip, my Phillip, was not only beaten, beaten to death, he was also violently sexually assaulted. So you see, your loving son Jason is not only a vicious, murdering thug, he's also a homosexual rapist... But perhaps that isn't perversion in your book. *(Exits)*

SALLY stands stunned for a moment, then laughs nervously.

SALLY: The man's crazy.

DAVID: *(To Perkins)* Is that true?

PERKINS: Yes, sir, I'm afraid it is.

DAVID: Oh my God.

SALLY: But you can't..?

PERKINS: Yes, mam, you can...

SALLY: But surely that's why they...?

PERKINS: Go to Samson Woods..? No, mam... As much as I disapprove of that sort... Just like a woman... You wouldn't say someone made love to a woman who'd been raped... And in the case of this young Phillip chap... It was pretty nasty, even without the hiding they gave him... And now the whole thing has turned as nasty as it's possible to get... Murder... And pretty violent at that.

SALLY: But Jason wouldn't... Jason couldn't... *(Sits)*

DAVID: *(Takes her hand)* What are we going to do..?

SALLY: *(Softly)* It's not true.

DAVID: But the car...

SALLY: *(Loud)* It's not true... For God's sake, do you honestly think Jason...?

DAVID: I don't know... I honestly don't know... There are a thousand things running through my head telling me it's all some ghastly nightmare... But every time it all comes down to the car... And that man who keeps phoning the police.

PERKINS: *(Sits)* I don't think it's helping none you two being at odds with each other. Maybe we're getting ideas into our heads that really shouldn't be there in the first place. Let's look at what we've got. A man gets beaten up. Another man sees it, does nothing to help the victim. Now that's odd in my book. Something doesn't quite fit the puzzle, so to speak... He phones us with the registration number of your car. Possible it was like the lady said, took the number of the first car he saw. Or, could have got the number wrong. You'd be surprised at how many times that happens. Then he rings up again. Says he knows where we can find the car. Who knows, Inspector Wyatt may now be down there on a wild goose chase. No car.. No nothing... Who knows... A bit of a puzzle that doesn't quite fit.

DAVID: You're forgetting something.

PERKINS: What's that, sir?

DAVID: He made a threat, you said.

PERKINS: Ah yes... Something else that doesn't quite fit.

SALLY: *(Stands, moves around)* Jason. Jason. Come home, for God's sake, come home.

Telephone rings startling them.

PERKINS: *(Stands)* I'll take it. It'll be Inspector Wyatt. *(Picks up receiver)* Hello... Yes Inspector... And, sir...? *(Very softly)* Yes, sir... I understand, sir. *(His expression goes blank. SALLY and DAVID become tense, suspecting the call to be confirming)* Is that wise, sir...? I will, sir... Difficult, sir... But I'll have to... Both of them..? Yes, sir... The station... Ten minutes... *(Looks at David and Sally)* No, sir, better make it twenty minutes... They have to get dressed... Yes, sir. *(Slowly puts receiver down)*

DAVID: Well?

PERKINS: *(His voice trembling)* Bad news, sir.

DAVID: It was my car?

PERKINS: Yes, sir.

SALLY: And Jason?

PERKINS: I have some rather tragic news, I'm afraid.

SALLY: Oh God.

PERKINS: The car was exactly where our informer said it would be... and... and... I'm afraid... I'm sorry but this will come as a shock... I think you'd be better sitting down.

SALLY: For God's sake, tell us.

PERKINS: The car had been driven into the wood, sir and was parked in a secluded spot... Sitting in the driver's seat was a young man and... outside... two other young men... I'm afraid...

DAVID: Was Jason one of them?

PERKINS: We don't know... We need you to tell us.

The following lines are spoken slowly, with a peculiar acceptance of the situation. Even Perkins struggles with the shock.

SALLY: *(Slowly)* You need... You mean..?

PERKINS: I'm sorry.

DAVID: They were...?

PERKINS: Afraid so, sir.

SALLY: *(Sinks into chair)* How?

PERKINS: Shotgun, we think...

SALLY: The man on the phone?

PERKINS: Yes...

DAVID: I don't believe... I can't believe...

SALLY: *(Softly)* Jason.

PERKINS: Inspector Wyatt wants us to go to the station...

DAVID: *(Softly)* Why?

PERKINS: Once they've done what they have to do, they'll be moving the bodies to the station morgue... I'm sorry, but we'll need identification... *(Pause)* You'll need to get dressed.

DAVID: Yes... Yes... Look, darling... I'll go... I'll ring Jenny... She'll need to be told... *(To Perkins)* Can we wait until Jenny gets home?

PERKINS: Yes, sir... would you like me to do it?

DAVID: No... *(Moves to the phone, dials. PERKINS sits next to Sally. She is in*

---

shock. PERKINS takes her hand and rubs it)

JASON enters

JASON: Evening all. Hello. Late night party?

DAVID drops the phone. SALLY stands. For a moment they stand staring at him.

JASON: What's up? My flies undone or something?

SALLY and DAVID both speak at once. Both rush over to him. SALLY throws her arms around his neck and holds him close.

SALLY: Jason. Jason. Oh my Jason. Thank God. Thank God. I knew it wasn't you. I said it wasn't you.

DAVID: Jason. Where have you been? Good God, do you know the trouble you've caused us...? Where have you been..? We've got the police here. Where have you been and where is my car...?

JASON: *(Shouting)* For God's sake, will somebody please tell me what's going on?

SALLY: Oh Jason. Oh Jason.

JASON: *(Noticing Perkins, who stands)* What's going on?

PERKINS: *(Stunned)* Jason? Jason Jackson?

JASON: Yes... What's wrong?

PERKINS: *(Adopts formal police voice)* Would you mind telling me of your whereabouts this evening?

DAVID: Where have you been?

SALLY: Jason. Where have you been?

JASON: Out.

PERKINS: Out where, sir?

DAVID: Where's my car?

JASON: Eh..? Look, one at a time... What am I supposed to have done...?

PERKINS: If you wouldn't mind...

DAVID: Leave this to me, Constable. *(To Jason)* Where have you been?

JASON: Been playing cards round Bunny Burrow's.

PERKINS: Since when, sir?

JASON: Just after ten. *(To David)* It was just gone ten, wasn't it?

DAVID: But Bunny only lives four doors up..?

JASON: *(sits)* So?

DAVID: You went in the car.

JASON: No.

DAVID: But you did. You stole my keys and took my car.

JASON: I didn't... Got my own front door key.

DAVID: Now listen, this is serious. So don't lie.

JASON: I'm not lying.

SALLY: Jason, tell your father the truth. As he said, this is very serious.

JASON: I am not lying. I have my own key.

DAVID: My keys were hanging on the hook in the hall and they're not there now. So, if you took my car, you'd better say so.

JASON: *(Stands)* They were not on the hook.

DAVID: Yes they were. And they're not there now. I haven't touched them and neither has your mother.

JASON moves to table, picks up jigsaw puzzle box.

JASON: They were not on the hook because they're in here. *(Shakes the box. There is the distinctive sound of keys rattling inside)* See. Now what's this all about?

DAVID moves quickly to him. Grabs box. Takes lid off. Lifts out keys.

DAVID: I'll tell you what it's all about. *(Turns sharply to Perkins)* Some bastard's nicked my car. *(Laughs)* Some rotten bastard's nicked my car. *(Sally picks up the newspaper and hits him around the head with it)* But my car! *(She hits him repeatedly as he protests, and the lights fade down to blackout.)*

BLACKOUT

THE END

PROPERTIES
ACT I

2 identical jigsaw puzzles of a country cottage

Newspaper (local evening edition)

Handbag (SALLY)

£5 note

ACT II

2 dinner plates

Remains of chicken curry and rice

2 earthenware mugs

2 water tumbler glasses

ACT III

3 teacups and saucers

Teaspoon

Sugar bowl

2 whisky glasses

3 coffee cups

Coffee pot

Set of car keys (inside puzzle box)

LIGHTING

Normal room lighting throughout the play

End of ACT I .... Quick blackout

End of ACT II .... Slow fade

Opening of ACT III .... Slow fade-up

End of ACT III .... Fade to blackout

SOUND EFFECTS

Door bell ("ding-dong" type)

Telephone ringing

Off-stage voices on other end of phone. (JENNY and PETER only - the audience does not hear Inspector Wyatt.)

Other NPN Full Length Plays by Simon Bamford

340 **Just a Loving Touch** 3M 3F

With only three weeks before the wedding Tony's life begins to fall apart. The bride changes her mind, his father wants to be Lord Mayor, his mother's sanity deeply concerns him and there's wallpaper to be hung. Help comes from next door - Heather, a young polio victim and her dad.

A touching drama sprinkled with Simon Bamford's dry humour.

317 **Scorpio** 3M 3F

Bill, terminally ill, is discharged from hospital. "He's been sent home to die", says Maud, his wife. "Sent home to enjoy the comforts of his surrounding family. What more could a dying man wish for?" Certainly not the unwelcome visitor who brutally forces them to face the truth of their lives. A violent, sometimes funny, moving drama.

Ask for NPN Plays by name!!!!